ABOVE & BELOW

PYRAMIDS, STARS, AND THE HUMAN SEARCH FOR MEANING

Tina Ketch

ABOVE & BELOW
PYRAMIDS, STARS, AND THE HUMAN SEARCH FOR MEANING

ISBN: 979-8-9937372-2-5
eISBN: 979-8-9937372-3-2

This work presents historical, anthropological, and cultural material for general information and reflection. It is not a manual of spiritual practice, divination, medicine, or legal advice. The author and publisher have made every effort to distinguish between documented evidence and matters of belief or interpretation.

We use BCE/CE for dates. Names and terms follow widely accepted scholarly transliterations where applicable. Respect for Indigenous communities is central; ceremonial knowledge identified by keepers as restricted is not reproduced here.

For information, inquiries, or permissions, contact:

https://TinaKetch.com
TinaKetch@me.com
https://YouTube.com/TinaKetch

DEDICATION

For every seeker who has ever looked to the heavens and felt a quiet stirring within, and for every wanderer who has stood before ancient stone and sensed a story waiting to be remembered.

To those who question, to those who listen, and to those who dare to believe that the mysteries above and the mysteries below were never meant to be separate.

This book is dedicated to you.

May these pages inspire you to explore the vastness of your own inner landscape, to honor the wisdom of those who came before, and to trust that your journey, no matter how winding or uncertain, is leading you toward the place where your truth resides.

Above, below, and within, may you keep seeking with an open heart, and may you discover the path that calls uniquely to you.

TABLE OF CONTENTS

PREFACE

A line divides the world: sky above, earth below. For as long as we have kept company with firelight and with one another, we have looked upward for signs and downward for roots. We studied the slow grammar of the planets and gave them stories; we stacked stone into mountains and wrote our hopes into the seams between blocks. We hid from heat or conquest in rooms carved underground. We asked cards and palms to speak back to us when language faltered. Through time and across places, humans have done what humans do best: we make meaning.

This book began with a simple wish: one history for one humanity that does not flatten differences into sameness, nor wall cultures off into silos. It listens to creation hymns beside climate graphs, to temple inscriptions beside work-gang graffiti, to Indigenous protocols beside museum labels, to star tables beside tarot pips. It treats a pyramid as both engineering and symbol; a mountain as both geology and kin; an underground city as both refuge and design. It refuses the choice between "myth or measurement" and instead braids story, evidence, and living practice.

Because a braid is stronger than a single strand, a few promises shape these pages:

- Many voices, one planet. No culture is the default. Traditions from Africa, the Americas, Asia, Europe, and Oceania stand side by side.
- Respect and clarity. Sacred stories are presented on their own terms. Where the historical record speaks, inscriptions, radiocarbon, tree rings, and stratigraphy, we explain what it says and how we know.
- Belief and evidence in conversation, not competition. Astrology, numerology, tarot, and palmistry appear here not as instructions but as chapters in the human search for pattern.

- Place matters. Mountains such as Shasta are treated first as living homelands with caretakers, then as sites of newer metaphysical meanings. Antarctica appears as science knows it, ice, rock, lakes sealed from light, and as recent legend imagines it.
- Plain language. Jargon is trimmed to what you need to follow the trail. When we use a technical term, it earns its keep.

You'll notice a few recurring features. Short "How we know" notes pause the story to show the tools: how cuneiform tablets date an omen list; how ground-penetrating instruments trace tunnels beneath a plaza; how linguists map migrations; how curators date a tarot deck or a painted hand on limestone. Occasional "Motif across worlds" boxes point out themes that echo far apart, floods and first people, underworlds and sky-ladders, tricksters and healers. These are invitations, not verdicts.

Any book that claims a world's width has blind spots. My aim is not to settle debates but to make them visible so you can see what is argued, why it matters, and where evidence ends and conviction begins. When traditions disagree, I say so. When scholars disagree, I present their best reasons. When a story's power outstrips its proof, I try to name both the power and the limit.

A note on names and dates: I use BCE/CE, and I give places by widely recognized English names, alongside local names, where useful. Spellings of non-Latin scripts follow common scholarly practice; when variants are well-known, I mention them. Quotes from oral testimony appear with permission or from published sources; restricted knowledge, when identified as such by community keepers, remains respectfully off these pages.

If there is a single conviction animating Above & Below, it is that our species survives by sharing knowledge, labor, and meaning. We inherited more than genes: we inherited libraries of story and craft that reach from ochre prints on cave walls to golden domes, from quietly clever irrigation ditches to neutrino detectors sunk in polar ice. Reading that inheritance with care helps us meet one another without costume or contempt.

May these pages leave you with a keener eye for both the measurable and the meaningful. May they help you hear the conversation between sky and stone and recognize your own voice in it.

Tina Ketch

INTRODUCTION

Reading the World Above and Below

Begin in the dark.

The first library most humans knew was not a room but a cave: a chamber where breath fogs and fire throws moving orange on stone. There, someone pressed a hand to the wall and blew pigment, an act that said "I was here" and also "we are us." Nearby, the same hand sketched animals with lines sure enough to make bodies move in lamplight. The scene teaches three things this book keeps close: that pictures can carry memory; that places hold story; and that meaning often starts where light is scarce.

Then step outside. The night has its own library. Long before telescopes, watchers noticed the wandering lights among fixed stars, marked the rise of certain constellations with seasons, and predicted eclipses by counting. In temple cities along rivers, in Africa, Asia, and the Americas, people made calendars, aligned buildings, and argued about what the heavens meant: signs from gods, gears of a cosmic machine, or mirrors for human character. Whether you read those alignments as ritual, as astronomy, or as both, they tell us that the sky mattered.

By day, we built. In Egypt's Old Kingdom, limestone mountains rose block by block on the plateau at Giza, binding royal bodies to solar imaginations and to the labor and knowledge of thousands. In Nubia, steeper pyramid patterns patterned the desert in another royal grammar. Across the ocean, in the Basin of Mexico, Teotihuacán set pyramids as anchors for a city's civic and sacred life. "Pyramid" names a shape; meanings are local. Each stone mountain tells you what people thought the world demanded of them.

Sometimes the world continues downward. In Cappadocia, soft volcanic tuff gave way to multilevel cities, Derinkuyu and its neighbors, fitted with shafts for air and stone doors for danger, works of engineering and community under pressure. In Australia's interior, dug-out towns learned to treat the earth itself as shelter from heat. And in story, underworlds hold moral maps: Maya Xibalba, Greek Hades, Hopi emergence places, cosmologies that instruct the living.

This book sets these ways of knowing side by side. It is a history of how humans made sense of being alive by attending to what was above, stars, omens, gods, and the measurements of astronomy, and what was below, the ground that remembers, the monuments we raised, the cities we carved, the worlds we imagined under our feet. It includes living esoteric practices, astrology, numerology, tarot, and palmistry, not to prove or disprove them, but to understand their social work: how they help people narrate a life, hold a crisis, choose, or hope. It also includes modern mountains of meaning: Mount Shasta as both an Indigenous homeland and a 20th-century spiritual magnet; Antarctica as both a continent of international science and a screen for new legends.

Three questions guide every chapter:

1. What did people say and do? Myths, rituals, city plans, songs, objects, movements.
2. What does the ground, or the instrument, remember? Archaeology, geology, linguistics, genetics, archives, and laboratory work.
3. How did ideas travel and change? Along coasts, through deserts, via markets and marriages, with empires and refugees, by printing press and internet rumor.

Because these domains often blur, you'll see me mark the footing. When I move from a temple hymn to a radiocarbon date, I'll say so. When evidence is contested or thin, I'll tell you what is argued and why. When a claim belongs to belief rather than to material proof, I'll treat it with respect as a belief and name it as such. The goal is not to drain meaning from the world; it is to show how many kinds of meaning humans make, and how we can talk across them without erasing or sneering.

A brief map of the journey ahead:

- Part I: Deep Time follows earth and early humans, the long climate rhythms, the peopling of the planet, the rise of language and fire.
- Part II: First Stories, First Arts turns to caves and creation stories, to floods remembered in ritual and in silt.
- Part III: Rivers, Roads, and Cities looks at grain and governance, writing and law, and at the stone mountains we call pyramids, from Giza to Meroë to Teotihuacán to Cholula, asking what each says about power, death, and continuity.
- Part IV: Maps of Meaning gathers philosophical and religious traditions in conversation, Buddhist, Daoist, Jain, Confucian, Indigenous, Greek, Abrahamic, without a single center.
- Part V: Esoteric Maps & New Age Currents tracks astrology's different lineages, numerology's number-souls, tarot's journey from courtly game to reflective tool, palmistry's travels, the layered meanings of Mount Shasta, and the many underworlds, material and imagined, that culminate in a sober look at Antarctica's real ice-buried lakes and instrument-strung darkness.
- Parts VI–VIII follow the widening weave: ocean highways and land empires; collision and creation after 1492; the rise of machines and markets; borders and belonging; and our present planetary tangle of warming, loss, repair, and responsibility.

Why now? Because the 21st century is loud with claims. Some of them are true and hard-won; some are sincere but mistaken; some are designed to dazzle or divide. It helps to know how a pyramid was quarried and why a star table mattered, and also why a story about a hidden city under a mountain or beneath polar ice can feel more satisfying than a footnote. When we learn the forms of meaning our species has favored, we become harder to fool and easier to move toward care rather than contempt.

How to read this book: straight through, as a long walk; or by parts, following your curiosity. The "How we know" notes are optional; they exist for readers who like to see the scaffolding. The endnotes and image credits gather sources for further reading. You don't need prior expertise. You do need patience for difference and a willingness to let two truths sit together: that evidence is precious, and that stories, especially sacred ones, do work in the world that numbers alone cannot do.

If you are a keeper of a tradition or a scholar of a field and you find an error, know that any mistakes are mine and that correction is welcome. If you are a general reader, know that your instinct to connect dots is part of the human inheritance this book celebrates. The trick is to connect them honestly.

We begin where many human stories begin: with time older than memory and with a spark that held back the dark. Then we'll step toward the first footprints we can date, the first traces of paint, the first stones laid in courses that still lift the eye. From there, the path climbs and dives, above and below, until we find ourselves again at the edge of the present, deciding what kind of ancestors we intend to be.

Turn the page. The fire is lit.

PART I: DEEP TIME

CHAPTER 1

BEFORE US

Begin much earlier than memory, before stories found breath. In the dark of the galaxy, a star dies and, in dying, forges iron, nickel, and a grammar of heavier things. Shockwaves stir a cloud of gas and dust. The cloud collapses, spins, flattens. In its center, a new star brightens: our Sun. Around it, a whorl of debris sorts itself by heat, metals, and rock inside, ices farther out, until grains become pebbles, pebbles become hills, hills become worlds. One such world claims the third orbit.

Early Earth was not hospitable. The young Sun is fainter. The ground is oceanic crust, made and unmade quickly, a skin of black basalt that wrinkles, rifts, and from which volcanoes pulse. Asteroids and comets still arrive, the last echoes of assembly. In one catastrophe, a Mars-sized body, nicknamed Theia in modern telling, slams a glancing blow. The impact splashes mantle rock into orbit. Gravity sweeps the debris into a bright companion: the Moon. Tides will be its voice. The day shortens; the tilt stabilizes. The planet begins, at last, to keep time.

Water finds basins. Rain hammers hot stone and flashes to steam, then returns. Oceans persist. Between the planet's inner fire and the light from above, a rhythm forms: new crust rises at spreading ridges and is swallowed in subduction zones; mountains thrust skyward when plates collide; rain and ice grind them back to sand and clay; rivers carry those back to the sea; sediment buries carbon; volcanoes give some back. The carbon-silicate cycle, slow and stubborn, becomes a kind of planetary thermostat.

Earth cools enough for continents to coalesce from lighter crust. The sky clears from choking steam to a blanket of gases that, while alien to us, let sunlight warm the seas. Somewhere, perhaps along alkaline vents where warm fluids mingle with cold ocean, perhaps in sunlit shallows rich in minerals, chemistry crosses a threshold. Molecules learn to copy, and in copying learn to err, and in erring learn to evolve. Life's first signatures are tiny: carbon ratios tipped by metabolism; mats that trap sediments into domes; later, fossils of cells. The planet's surface, once shaped only by physics and geology, now feels the tug of appetite.

For more than a billion years, life has been mostly microbial: communities of bacteria and archaea writing invisible biographies across rocks and seas. Some of them learn to harvest light and split water, releasing a new breath into the world, oxygen. At first, oxygen rusts iron dissolved in the oceans, painting ancient seabeds with red and gray bands. Only later does it enter the air in earnest. What is medicine to some is poison to others. The Great Oxidation reorganizes metabolism; it also alters climate: methane wanes, a greenhouse curtain thins, and ice advances.

There are times when ice may have stretched nearly to the equator, "snowball" or "slushball" Earth events. White planet, dimmed by its own brightness. Yet volcanoes keep exhaling carbon dioxide, untroubled by glaciers. After millions of winters, greenhouse gases build up; the ice retreats. The world breathes again.

New plans emerge. Eukaryotic cells, larger and more complex, appear, some with mitochondria that were once free-living bacteria. Cells learn to cooperate and to specialize; bodies are possible. In the Cambrian, just over half a billion years ago, body plans bloom in a geological blink: shells, spines, eyes, limbs. Not from nothing, evolution's quiet groundwork was laid earlier, but suddenly the fossil record has a chorus. Oceans thicken with creatures that burrow, filter, bite, and flee; predators and prey refine one another: coral reefs, trilobite highways, and the first vertebrate experiments.

Life tries land. Mats of algae and fungus creep onto damp shorelines; early plants follow, then learn the trick of wood. Roots clutch soil, and weathering quickens; the air shifts as forests drink carbon and exhale oxygen. Insects invent flight. Amphibians waddle out of water and, later, their descendants seal skins, harden eggs, and walk the uplands. Swamps of the Carboniferous laid down peat at that time, which was compressed into coal. Oxygen climbs. Fire, once brief and rare, becomes a landscape force. On a map of that time, continents are drifting toward one another. Eventually, they knit: Pangaea, a giant stitched from many plates, with a single super ocean to lap its shores.

The making and unmaking of supercontinents tug climate between extremes. Deserts spread within the supercontinent's interior; coasts are storm-wracked. Deep in what will one day be Siberia, basalt pours from fissures for long stretches of geologic time, a volcanic flood that alters air and ocean chemistry. The biosphere shudders. At the end of the Permian, most marine species and many land lineages vanished. Recovery is slow. Yet from the survivor's ledger, new worlds grow.

In the Mesozoic, dinosaurs diversified across land, sea, and air. Conifers and cycads shape forests. Later, flowering plants and their insect partners spark new ecologies of color and scent. The continents drift apart; the Atlantic begins to open; familiar coastlines only begin to hint at themselves. Under tropical suns, chalky seas bank up the skeletons of countless plankton. Under quieter skies, muds settle that will one day hold the print of a feather or a foot.

Then another sudden page turn. A space-thrown stone, many kilometers wide, strikes near what will be the Yucatán. Shock and heat. Tsunamis race; forests everywhere burn; dust and vapor dim sunlight to a weak memory. In the long shadow of that impact, many lineages end. Dinosaurs that were not birds vanish from land; their avian cousins carry a different future. Small mammals, nocturnal opportunists under dinosaur eyes, inherit landscapes and learn new ways to be big.

In the Cenozoic, Earth cools by degrees. Continents keep their measured dance. India sails into Asia and pushes up the Himalayas, mountains so tall and freshly formed that they draw carbon from the air as rock weathers to clay. Ocean gateways open and close; currents reorganize; polar regions isolate. Around 34 million years ago, Antarctica glaciated; later, Greenland followed. Grasses spread across many continents, rewriting diets and teeth. On a branch of the primate tree in Africa, apes explore new niches; some walk more often on two legs. But that is not this chapter's tale. This chapter's task is stagecraft.

Part of that stage is the planet's heartbeat: swings of climate paced by changes in Earth's orbit and tilt. The axis wobbles like a slow top; the orbit stretches and relaxes; the tilt deepens and shallows. These cycles, combined with greenhouse gases and reflective ice, meter Ice Ages. From about 2.6 million years ago until the recent past, great sheets of ice crouch over high latitudes, advance, retreat, advance again. Sea level falls to expose land bridges, then rises to redraw coasts. Winds carry dust that settles in layers fine as stacked pages. In warmer interludes, forests return to places where tundra stood. In colder peaks, deserts spread and glaciers grind. Through it, species shift ranges, adapt, or depart.

The most recent interglacial, the Holocene, began roughly 11,700 years ago. It is a climatic kindness by human standards: warm enough, stable enough, wet enough in enough places for experiments with cultivation to hold. Rivers that wandered in Ice Age pulses now meander more predictably; floodplains fatten. In several parts of the world, people begin to tend plants and animals; in time, granaries, villages, cities, law, gods of the city, and the field. But the Holocene is only the last thin page of a very thick book.

This, then, is the ground under every later story in Above & Below: a planet that learned to regulate its temperature by moving carbon between sky and stone; a surface stitched with plates that carry continents like rafts; an atmosphere that changed composition because microbes learned new metabolisms; oceans that record the breath of ice and the sigh of volcanoes; living things that remake their world and are remade by it in return. In this light, a pyramid is a brief mountain; a city, a brief reef; a birth chart, a momentary map of a sky whose deeper rhythms were set by orbital mechanics and long-ago collisions. Brief does not mean small. It means: contingent, precious.

How we know (notes from the toolkit)

Deep time, kept by atoms. Certain elements in minerals decay from one isotope to another at steady rates. Uranium in zircon crystals ticks toward lead; potassium becomes argon in volcanic rock. By measuring parent and daughter isotopes and knowing their half-lives, geologists can date crystals and the rocks that host them. Some zircons are older than any rock around them, tiny time capsules carried into younger strata.

Rock time, stacked. Sedimentary layers accumulate with the oldest at the bottom unless disturbed. Fossils, if present, appear in consistent order globally. This "law of superposition," coupled with fossil succession, lets geologists correlate strata across distances and build a relative timeline that radiometric dates then anchor.

Planetary palimpsests. Magnetic minerals in cooling lava lock in the direction of Earth's magnetic field at the time they formed. Bands of sea floor on either side of mid-ocean ridges show symmetric flips in magnetization, proof that new crust is made at ridges and pushed outward, evidence for plate tectonics.

Ancient air in ice. For the last hundreds of thousands of years, annual snow in polar regions has compacted into ice that traps bubbles of air. Cores drilled through that ice preserve samples of ancient atmosphere and the ratios of light to heavy oxygen that track temperature.

Extinctions, written as spikes. A thin layer rich in rare elements or soot at a boundary clay; shocked quartz; tsunami deposits; global pollen shifts, multiple lines converging mark rapid global changes. For the end-Cretaceous, the crater itself lies under younger sediments, but seismic maps and cores reveal its outline.

Tiny messengers. Plankton shells and cave drips grow with oxygen and carbon isotopes in ratios that shift with temperature and rainfall, letting paleoclimatologists reconstruct curves of ocean warmth, monsoon strength, and ice volume back beyond written history.

Motif across worlds: When Sky and Earth Part

Across continents and centuries, many creation stories speak of a first cleaving, sky lifted from earth, light pried from dark, waters separated and named. Read alongside deep time, the motif is metaphor, not measurement; yet it rhymes with genuine thresholds: a disk flattening from a cloud, a Moon separating from debris, a crust stiffening above a hot mantle, oxygen prying new possibilities from ancient seas. The truths are in different orders, but both answer the felt need for a beginning.

We end this chapter with the ground cooled, the seas salted, the air mixed by millions of small lives, the continents drifting under a temperate sun, and the planet breathing to the slow dance of its orbit. Readers of Genesis will hear an older music beneath these thresholds, light from dark, waters parted, a seventh-day rest. This book keeps that music audible while it lets geology and biology carry the rhythm of process and time. In the next chapter, we turn from stage to actors, from geology to lineage, and follow one animal's long apprenticeship in this world: becoming human.

CHAPTER 2

BECOMING HUMAN

Morning wind moves the grass. Footprints stitch a line from shade to water, heel then toe, toe then heel, two feet, not four. A child steps inside an adult's track, copying. The ground remembers this lesson far longer than speech does. To walk upright is to change what a body can carry, food, tools, infants, ideas, and what a horizon can mean.

Early in Africa, millions of years before writing, apes experimented with new ways to be apes. Some kept to forests, some ranged through woodland edges and open country. Bones tell the slow story: pelvises re-shaped, spines curved for balance, knees angling inward to steady the stride. Jaws lightened as diets widened; hands stayed deft. A few million years ago, ancestors we group under Australopithecus were walking well enough to leave trails in wet ash that hardened to stone. Their worlds were not ours, but they carried ours inside them.

A new thread enters: stone. It is one thing to pick up a natural cobble to hammer or pound; it is another to make a sharp edge and keep the trick in mind. By roughly 2.6 million years ago (with hints earlier), people we call early Homo were cracking cores to strike flakes, portable edges for butchering, and scraping. These Oldowan tools are simple only to modern eyes. They compress a chain of acts into a few decisive blows, and they imply memory, planning, and social teaching. You don't learn a good strike from instincts alone.

Bodies and minds co-evolved with this new economy of edges. Brains enlarged in stages; childhoods lengthened; adults cooperated to keep slow-growing young fed and safe. The cost of big brains is high. The payoff is flexibility: you can change your niche by thinking, making, and sharing. Around 1.9 million years ago, Homo erectus/ergaster emerged, a long-legged traveler with a bigger brain, a narrower pelvis, and a body tuned for distance. These were the first of our genus to carry their fires and edges far beyond the African cradle, walking into Eurasia and leaving bones and tools as far as the Caucasus and Java.

Their trademark tool, the Acheulean handaxe, appears by about 1.7 million years ago and endures for over a million more, a design so iconic it becomes a fossil of thought: symmetry held in the mind, then in the hand. If you hold one, you can feel the rhythm in its scars, the way a knapper turned, struck, turned, struck, maintaining shape across hours of intent. The handaxe is not just a knife. It is a curriculum.

Fire enters the record as glow and ash. There are scattered signs deep in time, burned bone, reddened sediment, but by about 400,000 years ago regular hearths appear in caves and open camps across the Old World. Fire buys tender calories from tough foods, warmth in high latitudes, light for evenings when stories stretch muscles you can't see. Fire also pushes people into tighter circles: you sit, you share, you watch sparks climb into the night, and you tell what happened and what might.

Evolution seldom proceeds as a single line. In Eurasia, another branch, Neanderthals, adapts to cold forests and steppe with sturdy frames and subtle minds. They haft stone to wood with tar they learned to distill, tended fire, used pigments, shaped bone and shell, hunted large game, and likely cared for their injured. In Asia, cousins we call Denisovans left so little bone that their genome tells us more than their skeletons do. Our lineage, Homo sapiens, appears in Africa by roughly 300,000 years ago (with fossils and tools that map a wide, varied homeland). "Becoming us" was not a lightning strike but a drawn-out workshop across many regions.

In Africa's Middle Stone Age, the tool kit diversifies: prepared-core techniques that produce predictably shaped flakes, thin points made for hafting, heat-treated stones that knap like glass, bone tools honed to tasks. People collect and grind pigments, engrave abstract patterns on ochre and bone, string seashells into beads, and beautify bodies and spaces. Whether you label these traces "symbolic," they do signal new kinds of attention, to materials, to marks that outlast a day, to the social power of display.

Language is the softest artifact; it does not fossilize. Yet the scaffolding for fluent speech, breath, brain timing, tongue and lip control, was in place in our lineage by the time our species cohered. The evidence points less to a sudden invention than to a deepening need to coordinate hunts, to negotiate marriages between bands, to teach a skill too intricate for pantomime, to soothe a child, to sing. Traditions shaped by Genesis tell the same moment this way: dust lifted by breath, a commission to tend and to name. Our toolkits differ, larynx and cortex here, garden and word there, but the work they describe is recognizably human.

We met our cousins on the road. As small bands of Homo sapiens fanned outward from Africa, likely in pulses beginning earlier than 70,000 years ago and certainly by then, they sometimes interbred with Neanderthals and Denisovans. That legacy persists: many people today carry genetic traces from those meetings, a record written in cells rather than ink. Exchange was not only genetic. Techniques and ornaments and pigments move along social ties that stretch for hundreds of kilometers. A blade core knapped here shows up there; a bead style travels across rivers; knowledge crosses as easily as obsidian when people meet, marry, and visit.

By at least 65,000 years ago, humans reached Sahul (the joined Ice Age continent of Australia and New Guinea), a feat that implies watercraft and wayfinding across island chains. In Europe and island Southeast Asia, people painted and stenciled deep cave walls and cliff faces, coaxing animals and signs from mineral and breath. In Siberia and later the Americas, people followed game and coastlines into new continents; by at least 15,000–16,000 years ago (with growing evidence of earlier presence in some places), bands were living from tundra to tropical forest in the Western Hemisphere.

Oceans, once barriers, became highways; coasts stitched worlds together.

What did daily life feel like? Much of it was ordinary genius. People built shelters and windbreaks, sewed tailored clothing with bone needles, wove baskets, stored seeds, ground pigments, cooked, laughed, argued, mourned, and taught. They tracked seasons with a precision born of hunger and care; they managed fire on purpose; they burned patches to flush game and encourage useful plants. They buried some of their dead with attention, grave goods laid beside a child; pigment dusting a body. They returned to certain places again and again because those places held water, animals, stories, or the bones of kin. Camp by camp, generation by generation, they tuned themselves to landscapes that were changing under Ice Age pulses.

If Chapter 1 was stagecraft, this chapter is the cast rehearsal. Muscles, minds, and social tools matured together until an animal with an ape's hands and a planet's curiosity stood ready to knit wide territories into networks of memory. By the time the last great ice sheets retreated, our species had become what it remains: a walker and a rememberer, a maker of edges and of songs, a creature that reads both sky and stone and turns them into meaning.

How we know (notes from the toolkit)

Footprints & bones. Trackways preserved in ash or mud record gait, group composition, and even play; skeletons show how pelvis, spine, knee, and foot adapted to bipedalism. Tooth enamel and jaw shape record diet shifts over time.

Tools that teach. Stone artifacts preserve the sequence of blows in their scars. Refitting broken flakes back onto a core lets archaeologists reconstruct the gesture order, evidence of planning and instruction. Use-wear and residue on edges reveal tasks (butchery, hide scraping, plant cutting).

Fire signatures. Microscopic changes in heated stone, ash layers, reddened sediments, charred bone, and magnetic traces in hearth soils distinguish controlled fires from wild ones and identify hearths used repeatedly.

Dating the invisible. Radiocarbon dates organic remains to roughly 50,000 years; beyond that, luminescence dating clocks the last time grains saw sunlight; argon methods date volcanic layers that bracket sites.

Ancient DNA. Genetic fragments from bones and teeth (and traces in living people) map kinships, migrations, and interbreeding; they can also flag past adaptations (to altitude, starch, cold, pathogens).

Small clues, big worlds. Starches and phytoliths trapped in dental calculus, isotopes in bone collagen, and strontium signatures in teeth reveal diets and movements; pigments and beads speak to display and social identity; tar and resins prove adhesives and compound tools.

Motif across worlds: First People, First Teachers

In many traditions the first people are formed, of clay, maize, breath, or word, and then **taught**: by animals, by ancestors, by gods, by the land itself. Read against the archaeological record, the motif honors a truth about our species: we survive by instruction. Walking upright, cracking cores, catching sparks, stitching hides, memorizing routes, the curriculum of becoming human was long, shared, and endlessly retold at the edge of the fire.

CHAPTER 3

CAVE WALLS AS LIBRARIES

Fire hushes a chamber differently than daylight does. The ceiling lowers, the world narrows to the oval of flame, and stone begins to answer with echoes. Someone dips a chewed twig or a wad of hair into ochre ground with fat. Someone else cups pigment in the mouth and blows around a splayed hand, one breath, then another, leaving a negative print: presence by absence. In that gesture, two truths sit together: I am here and we are us.

Across tens of thousands of years and on many continents, people turned rock into memory. In Europe's deep limestone, Chauvet, Altamira, Lascaux, bison crowd horses and deer; lions pad through dark; a rhinoceros lowers its horn. In Indonesia's Sulawesi and Borneo, red hand stencils bloom, and animals, pigs, and bovids step into view. In southern Africa, engraved ochres and painted shelters extend the palette; in Namibia, small painted stones from Apollo 11 Cave carry animals in portable form. In the Americas, cliff and cave walls bear hands, herds, spirals, and tracks. Cueva de las Manos in Patagonia is a chorus of palms layered by generations. The record is global; the persistence, astonishing.

What were caves for?

Not houses, mostly. The decorated chambers often lie far from living floors and hearths used for everyday work. They feel more like intervals, spaces set apart for initiation, instruction, healing, petition, remembrance. We cannot interview the painters; we can read the habits they left.

- Teaching and transmission. A painted herd is a field guide, a lesson in anatomy and behavior: winter pelts, rutting postures, wounded flanks. Dots and tally marks near animals may count hunts, seasons, or something we can no longer name.

- Ritual and relation. Some panels occupy acoustically lively rooms where a shout booms and a drum thrums. Many images sit where rock bulges and cracks suggest shoulders, haunches, snouts; artists coaxed forms from the wall rather than merely onto it.
- Threshold work. Hands at cave mouths and passage entrances suggest rites of belonging, "I crossed here," "we crossed here", and the making of group memory.

None of these uses excludes the others. A place can teach and heal, warn and celebrate. Caves, like temples, schools, and town squares, do mixed work well.

The craft that made the images

Pigments, ochres (iron oxides), manganese, charcoal, came from nearby outcrops or distant, prized seams. Ground on stone, mixed with fat, spit, or plant resin, they stuck to walls that still hold them. Brushes were chewed twigs, feathers, fur bound to sticks; fingers did their share; reed blowpipes or the mouth made even stencils. Painters shaded with hatching and smudging, used the wall's swell for a bison's belly, and scratched lines through wet pigment for hair. Torches and stone lamps, shallow cups filled with fat, threw a warm, flickering light that animated bodies; one step left or right and the flank "moved." Where ceilings run low, soot still seeds the calcite.

Tools lie nearby: grindstones dusted red, discarded "crayons," shell cups, flint for scraping films of calcite to prepare a panel. Footprints persist, adults, children, dogs or wolves in some places, along with palm prints and finger flutings in soft wall. These traces draw us close enough to see that the work was organized: certain panels revisited over the years; others respected as finished; paths cleared; lamps replenished; someone carrying in water or fat or stone.

Reading what we cannot translate

Interpretation invites caution. The popular phrase “hunting magic”, images made to conjure success, oversimplifies a record that includes animals seldom hunted, hybrids, signs, and scenes that read more like myth or law than a shopping list. Other frames, visions, shamanic travel, animal-persons negotiating with humans, fit some sites better than others and must be handled with respect for living traditions that guard such knowledge.

What we can say well:

- Animals are persons in many Indigenous and ancient philosophies. Panels that arrange species in ranked or facing positions may be telling relationship stories, not just inventories.
- Geometric signs, dots, ladders, chevrons, nested ovals, repeat across regions and centuries, hinting at a graphic vocabulary. We do not yet know the grammar.
- Place is the protagonist. Deep rooms, narrow squeezes, chambers with booming echoes, mineral “tears” that glisten, all shape what gets painted where. The wall is a collaborator, not a blank page.

Sister arts at the cave mouth

Even as painters worked in the dark, people carved and modeled in light: ivory figures with lion heads and human bodies; clay bison pressed with thumbprints; “Venus” statuettes that congregate in pockets across Ice Age Europe; beads and pendants strung as messages worn on skin. Bone flutes and whistles sound a music that could have filled those resonant rooms. Caves are libraries, yes, but they sit within cities of craft, villages of makers who stitched, knapped, carved, sang, and taught.

How we know (notes from the toolkit)

- Dating the undatable. Charcoal lines can be radiocarbon dated. Where paint lacks carbon, thin films of calcite that formed over or under the image carry traces of uranium that decay at a known rate; uranium-thorium methods bracket the minimum or maximum age. Context (floor deposits, lamp soot) strengthens the case.
- Microscopes and maps. Microstratigraphy reveals paint layers; pigment grain shapes betray sources; binders show up in chemical traces. 3D scans and photogrammetry conserve images digitally and reveal overlaps and corrections, evidence for planning or later repainting.
- Acoustics and movement. Researchers map echoes and resonances; some decorated panels correlate with "hot spots" in sound. Footprint trails and lamp placements suggest routes and rhythms of visits.
- Ethics and conservation. Human breath, fungus, and heat have damaged famous sites; many are closed or strictly limited. High-fidelity replicas and digital models let people learn while the originals rest. Local communities' perspectives guide access and interpretation where sites remain part of living cultural landscapes.

A brief tour by the light of a lamp

- A chamber of lions. On a limestone wall, outlines stack and pass, manes pricked, muzzles open. No arrows pierce them. The scene reads like observation, respect, or a story more than tally.
- A hand corridor. Left, right, child-small and adult-wide, some missing a finger segment, injury? Code? The passage makes a gallery of belonging.
- An animal over a bulge. The painter saw it first: the rock's swell as a shoulder. A few shaded strokes turn geology into muscle, the world's oldest relief sculpture.

- A field of signs. Ladders, chevrons, nested curves. No animal at all, just a page of marks. Someone rehearsed a graphic language we cannot read but can admire for its economy.

Motif across worlds: Hands That Say "We"

From Ice Age stencils to schoolyard paint to protest walls, the handprint persists. It is a signature and a surrender, a mark anybody can make that ties the individual to a group. In many traditions, handprints protect doorways, bless travelers, or witness vows. In caves, layered palms may have fixed an event, an initiation, a visit, or named a belonging. Whatever else they meant, they announced a truth older than writing: humans declare themselves together.

Afterimage

Step back, turn the lamp. The animals become abstract again, then vanish as soot and calcite take the light. Outside, the air smells of water and leaf. The painted chamber keeps its temperatures and secrets. Above it the sky records nothing, and everything, the drift of seasons, the long precession of the stars. Cave and sky are both archives; one stores the touch of people, the other the clock by which they measured return. Between them we first learned to bind time to story.

PART II: FIRST STORIES, FIRST ARTS

CHAPTER 4

MANY BEGINNINGS

Night falls; someone asks the oldest question: How did all this begin? Not when, that answer will come later with calendars and clocks, but how: with whom, from what, and toward what obligations. Across oceans and centuries the answers arrive in different voices. They do not cancel one another. They braid.

A circle of beginnings, a sampler

Aotearoa (Māori) Sky-father Ranginui and earth-mother Papatūānuku cling so tightly that their children grow in darkness. After councils and trying, Tāne pushes the parents apart; light floods the world; winds, birds, and forests take their places. Separation is not triumph alone, it is sorrow, too. Mists still rise from earth to sky like the embrace that was.

Yorùbá (West Africa) From Olódùmarè, the supreme source, an Òrìṣà descends on a chain, some tellings say Òbàtálá, others Odùduwà, carrying a snail shell of sand and a hen. The hen scratches the sand over the waters to make land; the first dry place gathers at Ilé-Ifẹ̀. Later, palm and people, craft and kingship, rooted there. Creation is practical: a descent, a handful of earth, a community built.

Diné / Navajo (Southwest North America) People and Holy People journey upward through layered worlds. Each world teaches and corrects, and after harms are repaired, the people emerge into Diné Bikéyah, the glittering world. With emergence comes ceremonies to keep the balance and stories to remember what is unbalanced.

Vedic (South Asia) In hymns, a Hiraṇyagarbha, a golden embryo, rests on primal waters before breaking into heaven and earth. In another song, the Puruṣa, a cosmic person, is offered in sacrifice;

from that body arise seasons and meters, animals, and social orders. The world is born from breath, sound, and offering; ṛta, order, becomes the frame that holds it.

China: A cosmic egg opens. Pángŭ grows between sky and earth and holds them apart until his death; his body becomes mountains, rivers, and winds. Later, Nǚwā mends a broken sky with five-colored stones and shapes people from clay. Culture heroes then teach farming, silk, and writing. Creation is separation, repair, and craft.

Mesopotamia: from mingled waters, Apsû (fresh) and Tiamat (salt), the gods arise and quarrel. In Babylon's telling, Marduk defeats Tiamat and forms heaven and earth from her body; order follows conquest; a calendar follows order. The city's ritual year retells this, making a promise that chaos can be faced again.

Kemet / Ancient Egypt In Heliopolis, Atum lifts from the primeval waters (Nun) and brings forth Shu (air) and Tefnut (moisture); in Memphis, Ptah conceives creation in his heart and speaks it with his tongue; at Hermopolis, eight primordial beings stir the first mound. One land, many cosmogonies: word, water, and rising earth all take turns at the center.

Genesis (West Asia) "In the beginning", a single God calls light, sky, land, and life into being, names them good, and rests on the seventh day. Humans bear the divine image and receive a garden and a charge. Creation is speech, blessing, boundary, and sabbath.

Maya (Mesoamerica) Makers and modelers try mud people, too soft, and wood people, too hard, without hearts. At last, they need people from the Maize, who can remember and speak. The world is not complete until beings live who can give thanks. The Popol Vuh brings the Hero Twins through trial and ballgame into a cosmos with rhythms to match the milpa.

Aboriginal Australia (many nations, many tellings) In the Dreaming, an everywhen rather than a once-upon-a-time, Ancestral Beings sing and travel, shaping country. Their songs are maps; their tracks are rivers and ridges; their deeds mark places that require respect. Law is geography sung.

Norse between fire (Múspell) and frost (Niflheimr) lies Ginnungagap, the yawning gap. From meltwater rises the giant Ymirand the cow Auðhumla. Later, Odin and his brothers fashion the world from Ymir's body; the first human pair is carved from trees. Ice and spark, sacrifice and shaping.

In Japan, in the Kojiki, Izanagi and Izanami stir the brine with a jeweled spear; drops fall and islands form. From their union come more kami, including Amaterasu, whose light orders seasons and court. Creation is a family story; governance descends from it.

We could keep walking, Zulu, Ainu, Haida, Sumerian, Zuni, Inuit, and the chorus would lengthen. The point of the tour is not to exhaust but to listen for contrasts and kinships.

What beginnings do in a community

Creation accounts are instructions, not just explanations. They answer "Where are we?" and "Who are we obliged to?" in the same breath.

- They place people in a moral landscape. If the world begins with separation, there are proper distances and moments for bringing things close. If it starts with a repaired sky, mending is holy. If it begins with sacrifice, reciprocity runs through all things.
- They set rhythms. Shabbat rests; solstices tilt the year; first fruits and first rains cue offerings; ceremonies recall emergence.
- They tie people to a place. A hill that is a first mound cannot be just a hill. A spring where ancestors emerged is not a campsite; it is a relative.
- They shape language and law. Words create; so words bind. Oaths, vows, songs, and names inherit power from the creation speech.

Patterns that echo, and where they part company

Across continents, specific motifs recur:

- Separation of sky and earth. Darkness opens to light. A space for living appears.
- Ordering of waters. Chaos becomes river, sea, rain.
- The first mound or tree. Dry ground rises; a world-axis grows.
- Creation by word, breath, or song. Speaking makes; singing maps.
- Making from a body. A cosmic person's sacrifice yields parts of the world.
- People from humble matter. Clay, maize, wood, dust, humans as earth with spirit.
- Emergence through layered worlds. Movement upward, with lessons at each level.

And yet the differences are as instructive as the rhymes:

- Time's shape. Some worlds begin once and move toward an end; others cycle; others are always now.
- Conflict's role. Some orders arise from victory; others from craft and consent.
- The divine's proximity. Ancestors as neighbors versus a creator beyond; a parliament of powers versus one voice.

How we know (notes from the toolkit)

- Texts and tablets. Some accounts are written, on bark paper, clay, papyrus, skin, paper, and can be dated by script, borrowings, and commentary traditions. They show evolution within a tradition as schools debate and reinterpret.
- Oral literatures. Many traditions live by voice, song, and ceremony. Collectors wrote versions down, sometimes insiders, sometimes outsiders. Responsible use means recognizing that a written snapshot may not capture performance, restriction, or

local variants. Where communities identify knowledge as restricted, we do not repeat it here.

- Language families and loans. Stories travel with people and also leap across them. Shared plot bones may reflect deep ancestry, trade-route borrowing, or independent answers to common human needs. Comparative work is suggestive, not proof of a single source.
- Archaeology and environment. Myths are not lab reports, yet they carry environmental memory: floods on river plains; volcanic mountains that smoke; deserts where springs are law. We read with humility: correlation is not identity.
- Translation. Key terms, ṛta, Dao, mana, k'ó, do not fit neatly into English. In this book, we keep certain words and gloss them rather than reduce them to thin equivalents.

Notes on words and respect

"Creation story" can mislead if it suggests a fossilized tale, safely behind us. For many people, these are living maps, told at certain times, by designated voices, with obligations attached. They are not folklore to be mined for metaphors; they are law. Where a community's keepers have published or permitted versions, we lean on those; where they have said "this is not for books," we nod and pass.

A handful of beginnings, told as moments.

- The world is separated: A child's hands press against earth and sky and push; light runs like water into the gap; parents grieve and bless. The first wind starts.
- The world is spoken: A breath warms the air; a word lands; a horizon appears; praise answers.
- The world is mended: A being smelts five-colored stones and patches a torn firmament; rivers calm; cranes return.

- The world is offered: A great body becomes mountain, river, season; those who eat and breathe owe the world back.
- The people emerge: A line climbs from one world to the next; mistakes are carried and corrected; songs are given to keep the way.

Why beginnings endure

Because they give meaning before measurement and belonging before borders, a creation account teaches a child how to greet a place, how to repair a harm, how to keep time, and how to be grateful. Later, astronomers will chart precession, geologists will name epochs, and historians will count regnal years. Those are precious. But without a reason to care, calendars are muscles without a heart. Beginnings give the heart.

Motif across worlds: Clay, Corn, and Breath

Humans made of clay, of maize, and of breath are not three species but three emphases:

- Clay says: You are of the earth; be humble; dust to dust.
- Corn says: You are of the field; share; plant, harvest, and thank.
- Breath says: You are speech and song; words can make and wound; choose.

Together they suggest an ethic as wide as the planet: tend the ground, keep the feast, mind your mouth.

Afterimage

Close the circle. Night again. A voice, elder, auntie, priest, teacher, uncle, keeper, finishes a telling. The fire guttering is part of the story: endings belong to beginnings. Outside, somewhere beyond the roof or the trees, a sky turns in long rhythms still indifferent to our small camps and yet ideally suited to teaching us time. Inside, a child lies awake, repeating the steps: separation, mending, naming; the path between worlds; the hen scattering sand; the first breath. Tomorrow, that child will follow a parent to the field, the boat, the workshop, the river; the work will feel like an echo. That is the point. Beginnings are not far away; they are underfoot.

CHAPTER 5

FLOODS & OTHER WATERS

At dusk, the river sounds like breath. It slides past roots and reeds, brown-green with silt that will feed the fields, and then, without much warning in some years, it rises. Banks vanish. A tree trunk turns and knocks a house wall with a noise no one forgets. The same water that carried fish and boats now shoulders doors and drags fences. When morning comes, it leaves a silver of mud that will take root. Blessing and threat arrive together. No wonder so many people keep a flood story near the front of their memory.

River worlds

Rivers gave early cities their calendars and their tempers. Floodplains offered flat fields that renewed themselves, a road you didn't have to build, and a danger that kept engineers and priests employed. Where rains track monsoon and mountain, rivers keep time predictably; where storms rule, they surprise. Communities learned to bank, dredge, terrace, and pray, a practical theology of water.

In ancient Kemet (Egypt), the Nile's annual rise was counted and celebrated; low floods meant hunger, high ones brought repair. In Mesopotamia, rivers braided and shifted in silts that could both fatten orchards and swallow boundary stones. In the Indus–Saraswati world, cities planned for drains and runoff; in North China, the Yellow River's silt could lift its bed so high it ran above its plain, an upside-down river waiting to rewrite maps. People everywhere invented cataract gods and flood deities and made offerings to the rain.

A chorus of floods

Flood stories do not all say the same thing. They reflect river worlds and sea coasts, ice-dam breaks and typhoon surges, and also the moral hopes and fears of the tellers. A few voices in the chorus:

- Mesopotamia: In the Epic of Gilgamesh, the survivor Utnapishtim tells of a council of gods who decide on a deluge; a friendly god warns him to build a great boat and carry the seed of life. Rain comes, rivers and sea join hands; birds are sent out to test if land has returned; the boat rests on a mountain. In the related Atrahasis tale, the flood answers clamor; afterward, limits and rhythms are set so the world can endure.
- South Asia: Manu rescues a tiny fish who grows enormous and pulls Manu's boat to safety when the waters rise; the fish, Matsya, a form of Viṣṇu, warned him to bring seeds and the seven sages. Land reappears; the world is replanted. The story reads as a seed of law and gratitude.
- West Asia: Noah builds an ark on command, shelters pairs of animals, rides out the water, and receives a covenant marked by a bow in the cloud. The flood is less a meteorology lesson than a moral drama: violence brings ruin; a remnant survives and vows restraint.
- Greece: Deucalion and Pyrrha survive Zeus's flood in a chest; after the waters drop, they cast stones over their shoulders that turn to women and men, hard things softened into kin.
- China (many tellings): A long flood, or a chain of them, covers plains; the hero's first answer fails; his son Yusucceeds by channeling rather than damming, dredging rather than simply stopping, a charter for water governance that endures: work with the flow, not only against it.
- Mesoamerica: In the Popol Vuh, the "wooden people" fail at gratitude and are swept away in a watery catastrophe before maize people are formed. In Central Mexican traditions of the suns (world ages), one end comes by water.

- Oceania & the coasts: Islands remember sea surges as gods in bad tempers or as lessons against arrogance: a reef overleapt, a taboo broken, a canoe lashed too late. In some Pacific and Indian Ocean communities, stories that once sounded like parables now read like tsunami manuals: if the sea pulls back suddenly, run uphill.
- The Americas (north and south): From the Northwest Coast to the Andes and the Amazon, people tell of waters that rise and rafts that save; of tricksters whose pride drowns a village; of twins or siblings who climb a tree or a mountain with seeds and fire.

The details vary: which mountain, which bird, which god, which kind of boat. The functions rhyme: remember, repair, re-begin.

What floods do in a story

Floods reset a world. They wash the board and demand that people restate how they will live with one another and the nonhuman neighbors they have. A few constant jobs these stories perform:

- Memory device. In river worlds, the flood is not hypothetical. A story teaches you what to do and what to store: seeds, tools, a list of animals; how to lash; where to head. The narrative turns disaster into a checklist disguised as myth.
- Moral audit. Many flood tales connect social breakdown, violence, mockery of law, loudness without care, to the water's rise. Whether or not a particular storm cares what we do, the story keeps accountability close.
- Engineering charter. Some traditions celebrate those who canalize, terrace, and dredge, making water a citizen rather than a tyrant. The hero is a surveyor with a ritual toolkit.
- New covenant. After the waters fall, agreements are renewed: with gods, with animals, with neighbors downstream. People mark time differently: a new calendar, a new first fruit, a promise stitched to a rainbow or a temple stone.

Waters other than rivers

Not all floods are brown water from a bankful river. Some are outburst floods: a glacier's tongue dams a valley until the ice fails, and water roars out in hours, carving coulees and rolling house-sized boulders like toys. Some are storm surges where low pressure and wind heap the sea onto land; some are monsoon failures followed by mad compensations; some are earthquake-slumped lakes; some are tsunamis from seafloor jolts.

Communities read these differences in their own grammars. A river people might tell of a god who sleeps through his appointed season and wakes in rage, or of a spirit offended by noisy feasts. A coast people might name a great fish turning in its sleep or a canoe god recalling his own place. The metaphor is local, the instruction global.

How we know (notes from the toolkit)

- Mud as a memory stick. Sediment cores from floodplains and deltas show thick layers of coarse grains between thinner annual deposits, paleo flood hydrology, letting scientists estimate the size and timing of ancient floods.
- Tsunami signatures. Storms and tsunamis both move sand, but tsunamis often leave distinctive sheets of marine sand inland, mixed with shells and sometimes ripped-up turf, in quiet back-barrier marshes. Layers recur where coasts have a long rhythm of great earthquakes.
- Tree rings & caves. Droughts and deluges leave patterns in tree rings, narrow for hard years, wide for wet, and in cave speleothems (stalagmites and stalactites), whose oxygen isotopes and growth bands track rainfall.
- Written gauges. Nilometers carved with marks and steps; chronicle entries of cities drowned; tax records that track harvest shortfall: texts that make water a number and a law.

- Landscapes carved too fast. Giant ripple marks, scoured canyons, stranded boulders in places where no modern stream could carry them: signatures of outbursts when ice-dammed lakes failed at the end of an Ice Age.
- Oral histories with time-depth. When stories about a certain headland's wave are held by communities across generations and match inland sand sheets and offshore quake histories, we learn to hear oral tradition as a precision instrument, not just a mood.

What we do not have is evidence for a single, global deluge in the time of cities that scrubbed all lands at once. What we do have is a planet that floods in many places and ways, often enough to keep flood stories close.

Boats, birds, seeds

Across distant traditions, a small bundle of motifs travels easily because it solves a human problem elegantly:

- The boat is a world in miniature, family, animals, tool kit, seeds, fire, songs, held inside planks and prayer. It is portable arkitecture: a shelter that floats and a community that remembers.
- The bird is a scout when eyes fail, raven, dove, or gull, sent to learn what water hides. A returning beak with a leaf is almost a valve between worlds.
- The seed is the future reduced to weight you can carry. After water leaves, it unfolds the old land inside the new silt. Whether myth names it explicitly or not, the bundle is always somewhere in the boat.

Water's double gift

Floods terrify not just because they drown, but because they reshape. They tear out old boundaries and redraw wealth: soils shift, channels move, islands appear. The next growing season in a floodplain is often the best one, so long as people survive to plant. This is water's paradox: destruction as preparation. Many rites of renewal, new year floods, first baths, river processions, honor this double gift. Many taboos, don't build here; leave that ditch clear; keep that grove standing, remember the rules that make the gift likely and survivable.

A short walk along three banks

- A tall stone with shallow marks. Children play at the foot of a stepped well on a river island where someone long ago carved height marks and dates. It is a calendar cut into a wall, a tax receipt, a set of warnings. Old hands lean on the stone in late summer and tell what each notch meant.
- A delta village. Houses on stilts keep kitchen floors above last year's high; boats are tied like extra rooms; a grandmother stores rice seed in a clay jar that moved in when her mother did. A new embankment shines where last year's failed.
- A far north coulee. Wind slaps grass that grew where water once ran fast enough to roll boulders. A geologist squats, fingers the varnish on a black rock, and sketches arrows in a notebook; a local rancher tells how spring runoff still tries that path after heavy snow winters. Two scales of flood, one landscape.

Motif across worlds: After the Waters

Across flood stories, the most important part is not the rain. It is the after: a bird let go; a ramp opened; a first step into mud; a first fire; a first offering; a promise, the kind you tie to your children's names. In some traditions, a bow in the cloud reminds both heaven and earth to keep restraint; in others, a canal does the same job. Either way, the after is law. "Again," say these stories, "but not like that."

Afterimage

The river falls back into its banks. Stranded fish flash; children shout; elders count losses and point to places that have long names like "Don't Build Here." Women and men shovel silt from doorways and set out seeds on mats to dry. Someone tells a story of the time the water was higher, of how an ancestor tied boats together and shared grain; someone else tells of the time it was lower, and we learned to dredge early. In a week, the reeds will be green. In a month, shoots will break the new earth. The flood's edge becomes a straight line on a wall where a parent's hand once set a mark for a child's height.

PART III: RIVERS, ROADS, AND CITIES

CHAPTER 6

GRAIN & CLAY

At dawn, a field is all dew and promise. A line of people moves shoulder to shoulder, sickles whispering through barley. A child runs ahead to chase birds; a grandmother tests a head between her teeth, nods, and hums a tune that belongs to this week and no other. By noon, baskets heap the threshing floor; by evening, grain rustles into jars. In the cool of the night, someone carries a clay token shaped like a cone to the storehouse and seals it with a cylinder engraved with animals and signs. A day's work becomes a mark in clay. Food becomes numbers. Numbers become rules. Villages begin to remember like cities.

The grain bargain

Farming was not a single invention or a one-way bet. It was a bargain, struck again and again in different places: more calories from less land, at the price of harder work, new risks, and new ties. Foragers had already managed landscapes with fire and favored plants along their routes. What changed, over thousands of years, not overnight, was commitment: tending, planting, protecting, watering, storing.

Independently and in their own tempos, people domesticated plants and animals in many regions:

- In the Fertile Crescent, wild einkorn and emmer wheat, barley, lentils, peas, and flax bent toward human hands; sheep, goats, pigs, and cattle joined.
- In China, millets in the north and rice in the Yangtze lands taught people the patience of terraces and paddies.
- In New Guinea, high valleys fostered taro, banana, and yam cultivation in gardens threaded with drainage ditches.

- Across West Africa, yams and sorghum; in the Sahel, pearl millet; in Ethiopia, teff, each with its rhythms.
- In Mesoamerica, maize unfolded from a grass called teosinte, with beans and squash as companions; in South America, potatoes, quinoa, and the herds of llama and alpaca shaped Andean lifeways; in Eastern North America, sunflower and seed grasses had their season before maize arrived strong.
- Along the Amazon, people enriched soils into deep black earths, terra preta, and tended orchards and fields woven into the forest.

Farming changed bodies and days. Backs bent more; teeth wore differently; diseases rode with crowding and animals; granaries smoothed the hunger curve but added the danger of theft and mold. In return, communities could grow large, store against bad years, support specialists who did not farm, and anchor memory in place. The bargain held often enough that towns thickened along rivers and coasts where transport was cheap and water routine.

River kingdoms of mud

Rivers supplied not just water but a building material that made cities possible: clay. From it, people made jars, bricks, tablets, and seals to guard them.

- In southern Mesopotamia, where stone was scarce and clay abundant, cities like Uruk rose in baked and sun-dried bricks. Canal webs fed fields; temples doubled as granaries and offices. Scribes pressed wedge-shaped marks, cuneiform, into tablets to track rations, fields, deliveries, and labor crews. The earliest writing there begins as accounting and only slowly learns to sing myths and letters. Cylinder seals rolled over wet clay turned a signature into a border of tiny art.
- Along the Nile, flood rhythms patterned calendars and taxation. Mud brick-built villages and palaces; papyrus-carried hieroglyphs where clay tablets did not. State granaries and

temple estates stored grain against lean years; scribes, thin reeds behind ears, became the spine of administration.

- In the Indus–Ghaggar-Hakra world, cities like Mohenjo-Daro and Harappa had gridded streets and ran drains beneath them. Brick sizes followed standard ratios. Tiny square seals with animals and a short, undeciphered script hint at an order that preferred planning to spectacle.
- In northern China's loess lands and along the Yangtze, people cut cave-houses into loess cliffs and raised rammed-earth walls; rice paddies mirrored the sky; later bronze-working elites would inscribe oracles on bone and shell as writing learned another path.

Where stone was handy, cities turned to it for temples and walls, but clay still underwrote the ledgers of daily life. Even where writing took other forms, the bark-paper codices of Mesoamerica, the knotted khipu cords of the Andes, jars and bricks kept time with their own quiet measures.

From tokens to tablets: how numbers became words

Long before the full script, people shaped clay tokens, cones, spheres, disks, each form standing for a measure of grain, a jar of oil, a sheep. To keep them together, they sealed tokens in hollow clay envelopes (bullae) and marked the outside with the shapes inside. At some point, clerks realized they could skip the tokens and press the signs directly into a tablet: faster, lighter, easier to stack. Numerals and commodity signs came first; names and verbs were latecomers.

This matters because cities are machines for remembering strangers. In a village, faces and favors track themselves. In a city, a warehouse needs lists. Clay gave memory a hard skin; writing gave it a time signature. What began as a tally could become a hymn; what began as a receipt could become law.

The house, the temple, the office

Agriculture grew institutions:

- Houses grew into lineages: compounds with courtyards, ovens, looms, storage bins, and graves under floors. Work tallied by birth and marriage moved within walls.
- Temples gathered offerings, stored grain, and employed craftspeople; gods took credit for canals and good floods; priests took measurements and kept calendars.
- Palaces and offices counted, levied, and redistributed. The world of weights and measures, standard jars, shekel weights, cubits, and cords, arrived with officials to enforce them.

With institutions came stratification. Some households could call on others' labor; some people were bound by debt or capture; some were free to adopt trades and move. In many places, women's work in brewing, weaving, and marketing tied houses to the city's pulse and, in some eras, to temple economies. Power-patterned space: ziggurats rose over workmen's quarters; elite cemeteries kept their distance; drains ran better near the center.

Irrigation, risk, and repair

Water on a schedule is salvation and a trap. Irrigation promises second harvests and orchards where scrub once flickered; it also salts soils if poorly managed. In parts of southern Mesopotamia, long centuries saw wheat give way to barley, hardier in salty fields. Dikes demand constant care; canals silt; floods rearrange. Cities thrived where maintenance became a habit and a law, corvée labor called up to dredge and patch; seasonal calendars posted like contracts between river and people.

Elsewhere, people learned other water grammars: terrace walls stepping Andean slopes; small weirs on African streams; qanats, underground channels, tapping Iranian aquifers; rice paddies stitching hillsides into mirrors. Each system braided labor and law into the landscape.

Debt, law, and clean slates

Once grain wears a number, it can become debt. Borrowing against next harvests keeps houses afloat, and can drown them. Many early kingdoms knew the danger. In Mesopotamia, rulers sometimes announced remissions, clean slates that canceled certain debts and freed bondservants to reset the social game. In Egypt, periodic tax amnesties and adjustments played similar roles. Law codes, famous and less so, put prices on injuries, set wages, named penalties for cheating the measure, and protected vulnerable classes more in principle than always in fact. Clay tablets and carved stones kept these promises public, if not always observed.

Exchange on long roads

Cities widen a diet and a horizon. From early on, caravans and boats carried obsidian, copper, tin, lapis lazuli, shells, oils, and finished goods along river roads and sea coasts. Merchants learned seasons, the pulse of the monsoon in the Indian Ocean, and stitched ports into circulatory systems that would later feed empires. Traders brought news, gods, songs, and plagues along with metal and dye.

Why cities?

Because granaries need walls; because markets need morning crowds and afternoon shade; because craft thrives near other craft; because specialists, potters, smiths, carvers, accountants, priests, feed on one another's skills; because danger concentrates and so does safety; because ritual loves a calendar and a stage. Cities are risk concentrators and meaning amplifiers. They store food, law, and story, and, in good seasons, they make more of all three than villages can.

Yet cities are also fragile: drought, war, disease, salinized fields, silted harbors, or kings too hungry for labor can hollow them out. Many great names, Uruk, Mohenjo-Daro, San Lorenzo, Anyang, rise, shine, and dim, leaving plans traced in brick and ditch. Others move their centers upriver or to new coasts and claim old names for new places.

Three rooms in one day

- The threshing floor. On packed earth, cattle circle, hooves and flails free grain from chaff. A child winnows with a shallow basket, learning the wind's grammar, how to throw and catch the rain of seed.
- The scribe's bench. A damp tablet, a reed stylus, a list: "seven workers, beer rations, two jars; two oxen, loaned; fifty bricks delivered." At the margin, a doodle, an ibex, all curve and horn, because even ledgers breathe.
- The kiln. Heat ripples; stacks of bricks redden to permanence; a potter raps a jar and listens for the note that means no crack. Tomorrow, the jar will carry oil through a seal to a storeroom where a woman counts and hums the same tune the grandmother hummed in the field.

How we know (notes from the toolkit)

- Plants in the ash. Charred grains and phytoliths (silica bodies left by plants) survive in hearths and floors; their shapes identify species. Impressions of woven baskets and chaff in brick faces preserve vanished materials.
- Stable isotopes in bones. Ratios of carbon and nitrogen in human and animal remains fingerprint diets, more C_4 plants like millet or maize; more marine protein; shifts with status or time.
- Tools and wear. Sickles carry silica sheen from cutting cereals; grinding stones pick up micro-polish and starch granules from seeds; residues in pots reveal beer, dairy, oils, and stews.

- Architecture and drains. Street plans, brick sizes, and sewer lines reveal authority, planning, and maintenance habits; collapsed walls hold replayable endings.
- Tokens, seals, scripts. Sealed bullae with matching tokens inside prove how counting systems worked; sign lists track how numerals became words; cross-readings between scripts (where we have them) anchor dates and names.
- Burials and households. Graves under floors and in cemeteries map kin and class; loom weights and spindle whorls in rooms mark textile work; storeroom jars, benches, and ovens trace daily economies.

Motif across worlds: Bread & Beer, Jar & Seal

The everyday sacrament of early cities was a double gift: bread and beer. Bread made grain portable; beer made it safe to drink and sweet to share. In many places, beer wages paid workers; bread offerings fed gods and poor alike. The jar and the seal kept both honest. A sealed jar is a promise between absent people; the impression on clay says "someone is responsible." The motif persists: the office stamp, the notary's emboss, the password, each a modern seal on a jar we still call a file.

Afterimage

Evening cool settles. In the lane between mud-brick walls, donkeys drift past, their bells tattling gossip. A woman steps from a doorway with a bowl of soaked grain and a paddle that smells faintly of yeast. In a courtyard, a boy practices rolling a seal over wet clay, lifts it, and laughs at the procession of beasts he has conjured in miniature. On the skyline, a stepped tower climbs the air; beyond it, the river turns a last copper curve and goes dark. Grain has become law; clay has become speech. Tomorrow, the city will wake and count itself again.

CHAPTER 7

WHEN CITIES DREAM

On the spring new year in Babylon, the city woke to a ceremony. Priests lifted the sealed tablets, recited beginnings, and led the statue of the god along the Processional Way. A king entered the temple, handed over his scepter, and was struck lightly on the cheek. If tears came, it meant heaven still favored earth; if not, the city held its breath. Outside, crowds thrummed; inside, the gods, gathered in assembly, were said to decree destinies for the year to come. This is what cities do when they dream: they turn time into theater, law into song, and stone into promises.

Time made public

Calendars that once lived in the sky alone, moons waxing, stars pre-dawn rising, became civic property. Festivals tied barley to constellations, river levels to tax days, queens' funerals to laments performed on cue. In Mesopotamia, "day books" recorded eclipses and prices. In the Nile lands, nilometer marks governed grain and levies; in China, dynastic courts printed calendars with official beginnings; in Mesoamerica, interlocking ritual and solar cycles structured everything from markets to wars.

A timekeeper is a peacekeeper. When a city's clock is visible, on a stair of flood marks, a drum at noon, a bell, neighbors settle crops, debts, and weddings without blood.

Law with a stage

Clay and stone turned justice into something you could point to. Edicts and codes, some famous, many unsung, named wages, set penalties, protected or failed the vulnerable, and clipped the wings of creditors when they grew too strong. Kings swore to be shepherds. Judges swore to keep measures honest. Oaths fed the gods of law with the breath of those who spoke them.

Houses that remember

Temples counted, stored, and staged. Palaces levied, spent, and sometimes learned restraint. Tablet-houses trained scribes who copied lists, laws, letters, hymns, proverbs, and the sorts of math that build terraces and canals. Archives grew: baskets of tablets labeled by string and tag; rooms where a city's memory could be stacked, shelved, and, when flood or fire came, baked to permanence by accident.

The city of gods and people: the Anunnaki thread

In the lands between rivers, people spoke of a divine assembly whose decrees ordered both heaven and street. In Sumerian, the high gods of this council are the Anuna; in Akkadian the name often appears as Anunnaki, "the offspring of An (Sky)." Membership is not a fixed roll call across centuries, but certain names recur with weight:

- An/Anu, sky;
- Enlil, authority and air;
- Enki/Ea, fresh waters, craft, cunning help;
- Ninhursag, lady of the high land, birth and growth;
- Inanna/Ishtar, power, love, and war;
- Utu/Shamash, the sun who sees, justice;
- Nanna/Sin, the moon, time;
- later, Marduk in Babylon's ascendancy.

In some texts the Anunnaki dwell above; in others, especially later, the term is used for the underworld's great ones, another reminder that pantheons move with language and with city fortunes.

What mattered on the street was function. The gods were the city's grammar: each district, trade, and law had a patron; each rite declared that the human order mirrored a divine one. In the flood story of Atrahasis, an assembly decides on a deluge, then yields when compassion and cunning intervene. In the Epic of Gilgamesh, councils weigh the heroes' deeds; decrees shape grief and order. In the creation hymn Enūma Eliš, an assembly grants a leader, and the Tablet of Destinies, a symbol of authority, passes hand to hand like a charter you can hold.

Alongside assembly stood another concept, the me, orderings or powers that make civilization itself: kingship, weaving, wisdom, the arts, even strife. These were thought to be distributed, bargained over, stolen, or gifted, mythic ways of saying that crafts and laws are not natural; they are made and maintained.

"How we know" (Anunnaki & the archive)

Cuneiform tablets, hymns, myths, court records, letters, lexical lists, carry these names and debates. Cylinder seals roll tiny processions of gods over clay. School exercises list divine epithets and rank. The same cities that dug canals and stamped bricks also copied tales that argued about how power should be clothed, in mercy, in terror, in law.

Reception and reinvention: the Anunnaki today

In the last half-century, the word "Anunnaki" has been lifted into new mythologies, as lost sages, star-kin, or ancient visitors. Within this book, we treat those modern retellings as modern stories: meaningful to those who hold them, powerful in popular culture, but distinct from what the ancient tablets say about councils, laws, floods, and fates. Our task is to let both kinds of story be visible without confusion, original voices in their contexts, and contemporary longings as part of today's search for origins.

The theater of power

Processions, enthronements, first-fruits, royal weddings, funerals, public laments, cities rehearsed themselves in view. Ziggurats and stepped platforms lifted rites into the sky; processional roads stitched temple to palace to gate. Music, incense, and patterned steps made cosmic order walk the streets. Skeptics and believers both attended; everyone needed the calendar to work.

The city's costs and cures

Where people crowd, disease and debt follow. Cities learned quarantine and drainage, grain banks and debt remissions, guilds and neighborhood watches, the laws of fire and brick. They also learned to cope with droughts, invasions, overwork of soils, and rulers who mistook themselves for gods. Yet the city idea proved resilient. Even when walls fell, techniques endured, brick ratios, measures, ledgers, litanies, ready to be rebuilt when water and will returned.

Motif across worlds: The Council on the Hill

From the Anunnaki's assembly to Olympus and Asgard, from councils of ancestors at the edge of town to synods and senates, humans imagine order as a meeting, voices, arguments, votes, or decrees. The motif instructs: good order requires speech and consent; bad order hides its counsel. A city that stages its decision-making, even as theater, remembers that power must answer.

Afterimage

In a courtyard, a scribe smooths a damp tablet and copies a line that begins, "In those days…" A child passes, chanting a multiplication table to the rhythm of footsteps. On the Processional Way, workers reset a fallen brick where weeds tried to claim a seam. The king returns the scepter to his belt; the priest lowers his hand; the crowd exhales. For another season, the city's dream and the city's day are stitched together.

CHAPTER 8

MOUNTAINS MADE BY HANDS, PYRAMIDS AROUND THE WORLD

Dawn reddens limestone. On the Giza plateau, three pyramids lift the horizon: Khufu, Khafre, and Menkaure. Once, casing stones caught the sun so cleanly they looked like frozen light. Around them sprawled quarries, ramps, workshops, a village of workers, cemeteries for those whose labor became a kind of liturgy. The pyramid is a mountain humans built to talk to time.

One shape, many meanings

"Pyramid" names a geometry, not a single purpose.

- In Egypt, pyramids rose as royal tombs wrapped in solar and creation symbolism. Texts on inner walls taught the dead king how to join the imperishable stars; temples at their feet stitched cult, memory, and maintenance.
- In Nubia, the Kingdom of Kush, pyramids stood slimmer and steeper, clustered in desert light, royal markers within a distinctly African tradition of rule, ritual, and art.
- In Mesoamerica, pyramids anchored temple platforms and plazas, places for rites, markets, decrees, and drama. At Teotihuacán, the Pyramids of the Sun and Moon structure a city; at Cholula, layers upon layers of construction make a hill that hides the world's largest pyramid by volume; at Chichén Itzá, El Castillo stages the equinox in shadow.

The shared intuition is less theological than civic: lift a platform, fix a line, make a stage where the human and the holy can meet while the whole city watches.

Making a mountain

No mystery diminishes the marvel. It takes quarried stone or packed earth, alignment to chosen axes, and logistics, food, water, tools, schedules, and songs. Workers' villages, bakeries, breweries, and clinics hum near the sites. Engineers survey with cord and sighting tools; crews cut, lever, slide, and set. Whether ramps hugged a core in spirals or rose straight is a debate that the ground answers differently at different sites. What is constant is organization: the power to feed, direct, and honor labor at scale.

The sky's grammar

Many pyramids converse with the sky. Egyptians tied corners to cardinal points; processions followed the sun and the star. Mesoamerican builders oriented platforms to solstices, zenith passages, Venus risings, or sacred mountains. Alignments are specific: not every monument aims at the same target; not every story of "perfect" correlation survives a careful measure. The lesson is attentiveness, not a single global code.

Tunnels below, cities around

Under some pyramids lie tunnels and chambers, ritual paths, burials, drainage, or earlier constructions sealed and built over. Above ground, pyramids rarely stood alone: avenues, markets, housing, gardens, and small shrines made them part of living cities with taxes and gossip, grain and games.

Pyramids in modern minds

Stone invites projection. Over the last century, pyramids have been recruited to claims about lost technologies, global blueprints, or mystical energies. In this book, we treat those as reception history, revealing of modern longings, while keeping the ancient monuments anchored in the lives that made and used them. The worker's bread ration, the quarry's echo, the priest's chant at dawn: these are the surest powers we can still hear.

Three vantage points

- On Khufu's casing line. Your hand meets a surface once as tight as a page edge; a chip reveals chisel marks neat as calligraphy. Down-slope, the workers' town lies on an old floodplain, with streets, bakeries, and fish bones in drains. The monument's heroics rest on a village of skill.
- On the Avenue of the Dead. At Teotihuacán, the Moon Pyramid frames distant hills as if the landscape itself were part of the city's design. Markets buzzed here; incense climbed; ambassadors and potters learned each other's words.
- At Meroë in late light. Steep pyramids cast long, blade-thin shadows. Reliefs whisper names. Sand pools in doorways once bright with paint. The elegance is its own language.

How we know (notes from the toolkit)

- Dates & names. Quarry marks, foundation deposits, surrounding cemeteries, and inscriptions anchor builders and timelines. Radiocarbon dates bridle possibilities; ceramic sequences refine them.
- Labor & logistics. Workers' towns, bread molds, beer jars, copper tool caches, sickle blades, and animal bones reconstruct the economy of building.
- Survey & alignment. Tool marks, postholes, and corner trenches show set-outs; error patterns reveal methods.
- Hidden spaces. Geophysical methods, microgravity, electrical resistivity, muon radiography, map voids and passages without opening them; careful archaeology tests what the instruments suggest.

- Use-life & after-life. Reworking, robber trenches, secondary burials, graffiti, and later shrines show how monuments were reused, honored, or cannibalized.

Motif across worlds: The Ladder You Can Walk

A pyramid is a ladder made stone. In myth, ladders and world-trees stitch realms; in cities, stairs do the same work. Processions climbing platforms rehearse a truth buildings whisper: if you raise a place where many can look together, you can make a people. The risk is real: stages can lie. The hope is also real: stages can teach.

Afterimage

Evening cool slides down the faces. A kite draws an invisible triangle above the great stones; children chase each other's shadows on a plaza edge. In a nearby house, a woman taps a jar and listens for a crack; in a temple, a keeper sweeps stairs where feet have worn the middles low. The mountain humans made looks out at a horizon it has outlived many times. Tomorrow, the sun will strike its edges again and make a bright rule in the air.

PART IV: MAPS OF MEANING

CHAPTER 9

PATHWAYS OF WISDOM

A grove, a market, a roadside, a courtyard, wisdom often starts in ordinary places. A teacher asks a question; a student answers badly and is asked to try again. Someone writes a brief verse on a palm leaf or bamboo slip; someone else copies it, argues with it, and adds a note in the margin. A city hangs a bell to mark hours; a household lights a stick of incense before a shelf of books. Out of such scenes, whole traditions of thought grow: how to be a person, how to keep a household, how to govern without ruin, how to face loss, how to use power, how to die.

This chapter listens to several pathways of wisdom, South Asian, Chinese, Greco-Mediterranean, African, and Indigenous, without making any one the measure of the others. Their tools differ (dialogue, commentary, ritual, meditation, proverb), but their questions rhyme.

What counts as "wisdom"?

Not just cleverness. In many languages, the word blends knowledge, skill, and character, knowing what is true, being able to do what is fitting, and becoming the sort of person who can be trusted with both. These pathways treat the self as a work in progress and the community as the workshop.

South Asia, Renouncers, Householders, and the Work of Freedom

In the forests and towns of ancient India, two currents braided around the fire of dharma (right order and responsibility):

- Householders tended ritual and kin, kept memory, and anchored law.

- Renouncers (śramaṇa movements) stepped away, shaving heads, begging for food, testing what the mind can learn when it carries little.

From this conversation came a spectrum of practices and philosophies.

Upaniṣadic reflection (late Vedic): short, luminous teachings probe the self (ātman), the ground of reality (brahman), and the identity or relation between them. The question is intimate: What is the knower of this breath and thought? The answers are metaphysical and practical: restraint, attention, truthfulness, and training the senses.

Jain paths center on-nonviolence (ahiṃsā) to a radical degree, vows to avoid harm in thought, word, and deed; careful livelihood; fasting and meditation; a disciplined community that includes monks, nuns, and lay supporters. Freedom comes by unbinding the soul from accumulated action through vow-keeping and austerity.

Buddhist paths begin with diagnosis: suffering, its causes, its cessation, and the path, the Noble Eightfold Path (view, intention, speech, action, livelihood, effort, mindfulness, concentration). Impermanence and no fixed self are not despair but invitation: because things are made, they can be made differently. Monastic saṅghas and lay circles together cultivate ethics, meditation, and insight; compassion is a method, not merely a sentiment.

The household synthesis (e.g., the Bhagavad Gītā): duty without clinging, action offered without greed for the fruit, in the stream of family, work, and governance. It is not world-rejection but world-purification.

Across this field, you meet disciplines familiar from our chapter on bodies of breath: sitting, breath control, mantra, visualization, vows. The aim is not only to know reality but to be shaped by that knowledge.

China, Way, Pattern, and the Art of the Fitting

In early China, thinkers argued with an eye on family, office, and season, how to align conduct with the grain of things.

The Ru tradition (Confucian) puts humaneness (rén) and ritual propriety (lǐ) at the center. A person is not a floating unit but a node in relationships, child, elder, friend, subject, ruler, each with fitting gestures and speech. Self-cultivation (study, reflection, music, ritual) makes character; character makes order. Mencius sees sprouts of goodness in us, compassion, shame, and respect that need tending. Xunzi warns that goodness comes only through training against raw impulse. Both agree: the point is practice, not slogan.

Daoist voices (Laozi, Zhuangzi) praise the Way (Dao) that precedes and exceeds our schemes. They commend wúwéi(unforced action), flexibility, humility, and the art of not over-managing. Zhuangzi's butterfly laughs at fixed identity; his woodworker listens for where the grain wants the blade to go. Here, wisdom is easily aligned with reality, not passivity.

Mohist writers argue for impartial concern and utility, feed the poor, stop wasteful wars, and distrust ornate rites that drain the granary. Legalist strategists, facing warring states, harden law and punishment, institutionalizing suspicion. Later dynasties synthesize, with officials educated in Ru classics while drawing selectively from other toolkits.

The throughline is fit: person to role, law to season, action to context, human will to the larger pattern of the world.

The Greco-Mediterranean, Argument as a Way of Life

Around the Aegean and later across Hellenistic cities, philosophy became both public sport and private discipline.

Socrates asked questions that stripped false certainty; his "I do not know" was a method to make room for better knowing. Plato dramatized these encounters, exploring justice, love, knowledge, and the forms that intelligible reality might take. Aristotle built systems, logic, biology, ethics, and politics, yet anchored virtue in habit: we become just by doing just acts; the goal is eudaimonia (flourishing), a life of excellent activity in accord with reason, within a community.

Hellenistic schools turned philosophy into daily practice:

- Stoics trained perception and will: distinguish what you can control from what you cannot; align with nature's rational order; cultivate courage, justice, self-control, practical wisdom; treat all humans as fellow citizens of a cosmopolis.
- Epicureans sought ataraxia (peace of mind): limit desires to what can be satisfied simply; honor friendship; understand nature so fear of gods and death loosens. Pleasure means freedom from pain, not excess.
- Skeptics suspended judgment to escape dogmatism's anxiety.

Across these schools, you see handbooks, letters, exercises, meditations: philosophy as therapy, not mere theory.

Africa, Order, Character, Reciprocity

On the Nile, early instruction texts (e.g., the "teachings" of Ptahhotep, the wisdom of Amenemope) counsel truthfulness, restraint, generosity, and respect for the poor under the canopy of Maʿat, truth, balance, and order. Wisdom is measured by speech that steadies and deeds that fit a just pattern.

Far to the west and south, philosophies live in proverbs, praise poetry, ritual, and law:

- In Yorùbá thought, ìwà (character) and àṣẹ (effective, animated power) travel together: speech and song move the world when aligned with rightness; divination (Ifá) is not fortune-telling so much as counsel for decision.

- In Akan traditions, sankofa (go back and get it) figures wisdom as returning to fetch what was forgotten, memory as a guide for change.
- In parts of southern Africa, ubuntu ("a person is a person through other people") names an ethic of relational personhood, hospitality, and repair.

These are not footnotes to imported systems. They are theories in action, embodied in courts, councils, festivals, kinship, and art.

The Americas & the Pacific, Rootedness, Reciprocity, Right Relations

In Central Mexico, Nahua sages (tlamatinime) asked how to walk "on the slippery earth." The answer, neltiliztli, rootedness, well-grounded truth, comes through balanced conduct, good speech, and flower and song (art) that harmonize heart and community. Elders' discourses (Huehuetlahtolli) teach courtesy, restraint, courage, and craft.

In the Andes, ayni (reciprocity) orders labor and feast: help given now returns later; water, pasture, and terrace are governed by shared obligation. Wisdom is a calendar of mutuality.

Across Oceania, concepts like mana (potency) and tapu/kāpu (sacred restrictions) regulate power and protect life. In Aotearoa, tikanga (right practice) and whakapapa (genealogy) bind ethics to kin, land, and story. In Australia, sung songlines map country; to act rightly is to remember and enact those tracks with care.

In these traditions, the world is not a backdrop but relative; philosophy is what you do together, so relationships thrive.

Shared Questions, Different Grammars

Across these paths, certain questions recur:

1. What is a person? A soul, a process, a node in kinship, a role, a luminous emptiness, a citizen?
2. What is a good life? Flourishing, liberation, harmony, balance, service, peace of mind?
3. What spoils it? Ignorance, craving, arrogance, disorder, forgetfulness, unjust institutions?
4. What repairs it? Virtue and habit, meditation, ritual, law, friendship, reciprocity, truthful speech?

The answers diverge, sometimes sharply. That divergence is not a bug; it is the data. Traditions learned what they learned from problems close at hand: drought and court intrigue, conquest and plague, family sorrow and commercial temptation.

Technologies of Wisdom

- Dialogue: from Socratic streets to Buddhist debates, questioning as craft.
- Commentary: layered reading, texts surrounded by notes surrounded by notes, traditional thinking out loud across centuries.
- Ritual & etiquette: not pomp but pedagogy; repeated forms shape perception and muscle.
- Meditation & breath: training attention (see Chapter "Bodies of Breath").
- Proverb & song: portable ethics; truth you can carry to the field.
- Examination & office: schools, guilds, monasteries, institutions that stabilize and sometimes ossify learning.
- Friendship: circles of practice (sangha, fellowship, garden, grove) where ideas become habits.

Women, Outsiders, and the Edges

The archive often skews toward male, elite, literate voices. Yet the record still lets us glimpse: Gārgī challenging sages; Therīgāthā poems by early Buddhist nuns; Ban Zhao writing on learning and conduct; Hypatia teaching mathematics and philosophy; countless unnamed mothers, healers, poets, traders, and keepers whose proverbs teach more people than any court lecture. A fair history of wisdom names the bias and listens for the edges.

How ideas travel (preview)

Trade routes carry gods and arguments. Buddhism crosses mountains into Central and East Asia and transforms; Greek and Near Eastern sciences flow into Arabic, Persian, and Syriac, then back into Latin; African scholars at Timbuktu annotate law and astronomy; Sephardic translators in Iberia move ideas between Hebrew, Arabic, and Romance tongues. We will track these crossings in later parts ("Oceans as Highways," "Empires & Edges").

How we know (notes from the toolkit)

- Texts & commentaries: palm-leaf manuscripts, bamboo slips, papyrus, parchment, paper; canon formation and scholastic debate; how copying preserves and transforms.
- Archaeology of schools: monasteries, academies, libraries, examination halls, teacher's houses; writing tools and curriculum tablets.
- Oral literatures: speeches, proverbs, epics, collected by insiders and outsiders; performance context matters.
- Lives & letters: biographies, edicts, legal cases, and correspondence that show ideas at work in courts and kitchens.

- Comparative caution: cognate terms (e.g., “virtue,” “Dao,” “dharma,” “Maʿat,” “ubuntu,” “ayni”) overlap but do not coincide; we keep local meanings primary.

Motif across worlds: The Middle Way, the Mean, the Balance

Different words, similar posture: the Middle Way between indulgence and austerity; the Golden Mean between excess and deficiency; zhōngyōng (central harmony); Maʿat’s balance; pono (rightness). None of these are timid compromise. They are artful proportion, courage that avoids recklessness, generosity that avoids prodigality, speech that avoids both flattery and cruelty.

Afterimage

Evening. In one street, a reciter chants a sutra; in another, a teacher in plain robes bows to a tablet with four characters and begins a lesson on filial piety and righteous anger. A friend writes a letter about grief and recommends a practice: walk at dawn, notice breath, keep a small promise, write what can be controlled and what cannot. In a courtyard, elders trade proverbs across a bowl of food. None of them thinks they are doing “philosophy” as a separate sport. They are keeping a way.

CHAPTER 10

ONE GOD, MANY PATHS

The week has a pulse. On Friday at noon, a voice climbs a minaret and pours over courtyards; men and women wash hands, faces, and feet, and line up shoulder to shoulder. Saturday arrives by candlelight and blessing over wine and bread; a table becomes a small sanctuary where work relents and time widens. Sunday morning opens with bells or whispered prayers; bread is broken, or a psalm unfurls, and people file out into streets that look different for having been held. The three scenes share a claim as bold as it is simple: there is one God, and remembering that changes how a life is lived.

This chapter listens to Judaism, Christianity, and Islam in the world context, how they shaped law and kitchens, cities and calendars; how they braided love, justice, and power; how they argued, translated, and sang; how they met one another as neighbors, rivals, kin.

Scripture as a library, not a single book

Judaism. The Tanakh, Torah (Teaching), Prophets, Writings, is a library gathered over centuries: law and story, lament and praise, proverb and prophecy. Its voices keep company with a vast interpretive garden: midrash, Talmud, commentaries, prayer books, and legal codes. Study is a ritual in its own right; argument is devotion.

Christianity. The Bible is Hebrew scriptures read anew, plus the Gospels, letters, and other early texts collected as the New Testament, copied, ordered, and argued over in communities spread from Jerusalem to Antioch, Alexandria to Rome, Edessa to Ethiopia. Scripture is read in liturgy, chanted, and preached; it takes flesh in creeds, councils, and monastic rules; art and music become commentaries in color and sound.

Islam. The Qur'an is recitation: verses heard, memorized, and written, gathered into a book whose sound is worship. Around it grew hadith, reports of the Prophet's words and practices, sorted, sifted, and weighed for trustworthiness. Tafsīr (commentary) and fiqh (jurisprudence) interpret text for life, and the science of transmission itself becomes a craft and a conscience.

All three traditions treat text as a living partner. They canonize, copy, gloss, sing, and argue. They keep chains of learning, teachers and students, isnād and ordination, so that words can travel centuries without losing their spine.

Law you can taste and touch

These faiths do not live on sermons alone; they become habits.

- Time. A weekly rhythm, a sabbath, a Sunday, a Friday congregation, anchors days. Yearly cycles mark fast and feast: Passover, Easter/Pentecost, Ramadan/Eid; others gather harvests and histories, Sukkot, Ashura (for many Shiʿa), Advent/Lent, so memory sits in the calendar, not just in the head.
- Food. Kashrut and ḥalāl laws make ethics edible: blessings before meals, forbidden and permitted cuts, slaughter as a practiced mercy, and fasting as a calibration of appetite. Even where rules differ sharply, the message is shared: eating is moral work.
- Money. Almsgiving is not charity's mood but command: tzedakah, zakat, the parish poor box. Debt rules, interest debated, remissions proclaimed, waqf/endowments dedicated, tie piety to economic justice.
- Speech. Oaths matter; gossip wounds; truth and mercy fence the tongue. Law codes and counsel literature take the kitchen and market as seriously as the temple and court.

- Body. Circumcision and immersion, marriage and burial rites, clothing and modesty codes: the body bears covenant as plainly as parchment does.

The law aims less to discipline strangers than to train a people. A city sounds different when many of its households bless bread the same way.

God, empire, neighborhood

None of these faiths lived long as private clubs. They met empire, sometimes as subjects, sometimes as challengers, sometimes as partners, and learned both influence and compromise.

- Judaism lived through temple states and exile, the shock of the Second Temple's fall, and a long diaspora that made study, home, and synagogue the movable center of a scattered people. Minority life under many rulers sharpened the arts of adaptation and law.
- Christianity, born under Roman rule, grew from a persecuted movement into a state church; later it fractured and seeded many churches that partnered uneasily with kings and princes. Where the empire marched, missionaries and merchants followed, and sometimes preceded, planting monasteries, cathedrals, and village chapels from Nubia to Ireland, Armenia to Kerala, Axum to the steppe. Power made grand art and grave mistakes.
- Islam rose as scripture and polity at once. Within a century, it stretched from Spain to Central Asia; courts and markets, libraries and caravanserais stitched a shared civilizational space where scholars, artisans, and traders traveled. Non-Muslim communities lived as protected peoples with taxes and constraints; at times convivencia worked, at times it failed. Across centuries, Sunni and Shi'a communities grew, argued, and sometimes bled.

The three met in ports and frontiers, in translation circles, in marriages and markets. They traded books, words, and techniques, along with polemics and, too often, violence. The record is complex enough to resist slogans.

Translation, argument, science

Ideas travel with goods. Syriac-speaking Christians preserved and translated Greek learning into Arabic; Muslim philosophers and physicians read and critiqued it; Jewish and Christian scholars rendered Arabic science back into Hebrew and Latin. Observatories and hospitals, legal manuals and instruments, paper mills and libraries appeared in cities that could sustain them: Baghdad, Córdoba, Cairo, Fez, Samarqand, Toledo, and Paris.

Within each tradition, thinkers practiced philosophy as service:

- Kalām (dialectical theology) and falsafa (philosophy) tested reason's reach under revelation; jurists compared methods and schools of law.
- Rabbis argued cases across centuries, balancing text and precedent, equity and fence-building.
- Scholastics, in Latin West and Greek East, worked logic and metaphysics into handbooks for preachers and physicians as well as princes.

None of this erases the failures of curiosity; all three traditions have had moments of closing ranks. But the long view shows sustained effort to match intelligence to devotion.

The inner turn: mystic grammars

Everywhere, some seekers turned inward without turning away.

- Judaism's mystical streams coalesced in Kabbalah: symbol-rich readings of scripture, the sefirot as emanations, practices that weave letter and breath.

- Christianity carried desert prayer into chants and hesychast quiet, into women's visions and monks' ladders of humility, into mystics who wrote of love's dark nights and bright mornings. Icons taught seeing; silence taught speech.
- Sufism made remembrance (dhikr) and love its center: orders formed around teachers; poetry stretched language to hold longing; music and motion taught surrender and joy. Many Sufis lived inside the law's discipline and sought its heart; some pressed beyond and were corrected or condemned.

These inner grammars are not the same, but they rhyme: breath, repetition, service, awe; the training of attention; a refusal to let law go cold or love go vague.

Women and the page, women and the street

The archive names too few women, yet names some: Deborah and Huldah, judges and prophets; Bruriah, learned voice in the Talmud; Mary as theotokos in Christian councils and as mother revered in many churches; Hildegard composing visions and music; Perpetua, Macrina, Egeria traveling and writing; Khadīja, merchant and first believer; ʿĀʾisha, transmitter of hadith; al-Shifāʾ teaching literacy; Rābiʿa al-ʿAdawiyya burning for God; scholars, poets, businesswomen across markets and courts. Their work shows that the "people of the book" were always also people of households, fields, and shops, where wisdom is enacted or betrayed.

Splitting and mending

Unity proved difficult. Judaism's Second Temple sects shaded into rabbinic orthopraxy and groups like the Karaites who rejected oral law. Christianity fissured early (councils, creeds, East/West) and later (Reformations within Reformations), making an ecology of churches that still debate scripture and sacrament. Islam's early political fractures hardened into Sunni–Shiʿa differences with rich internal diversity (legal schools, theological trends, Sufi orders).

Each tradition holds mechanisms of repair, councils, synods, madhhabs, new covenants, and none has finished the work.

Art that teaches

A law you can touch needs art you can live inside.

- Synagogues carry Hebrew words in stone and mosaic; the ark faces Jerusalem; light and reading frame the week.
- Churches shape space for processions, sacraments, and seasons: basilicas like roads; domes like skies; stained glass as scripture for the eyes; chant teaching the heart.
- Mosques unfold courtyards and columns, niches that show direction, carved and painted verses that make writing a sanctuary; calligraphy and geometry teach that form can worship.

These are schools of seeing and moving, architecture as catechism.

Neighbor work

For much of history, these communities lived within sight of one another, sharing wells, markets, lullabies, and lull years. They borrowed and resisted, hosted and harried. The record holds pogroms and inquisitions, expulsions and forced conversions, and also contracts, friendships, marriages, scholarly partnerships, and long centuries of ordinary coexistence less dramatic than a war but more important than a decree. Cities that learned neighbor work, however imperfectly, lasted longer and invented more.

How we know (notes from the toolkit)

- Manuscripts & memory. Scrolls and codices, palimpsests and commentaries; comparative textual work that follows variant readings; oral recitation that stabilizes text and melody.

- Archaeology of worship. Synagogue floors and inscriptions; house-churches and cathedrals; early mosques and prayer spaces; cemeteries, mikva'ot, baptisteries, ablution fountains.
- Law in practice. Responsa literature (rabbinic letters answering real cases); fatwās and court records; canon law collections; marriage contracts, waqf charters, market regulations.
- Coins & calendars. Dating reforms, regnal years, festival cycles stamped in metal and carved in stone.
- Translation chains. Greek → Syriac → Arabic → Hebrew/Latin; Arabic scientific instruments and treatises crossing into monastic and university libraries; marginalia that show students arguing back.

And always: the testimony of living communities, whose rites and kitchens remain the best commentaries on old words.

Motif across worlds: Exile and Return, Stranger and Host

All three traditions teach that the stranger matters, "you were strangers," "I was a stranger," "the guest is God-sent", and that home is a promise kept by memory, law, and mercy. Exile and return, journey and welcome, are rhythms deeper than politics. Cities that remember them are kinder; empires that forget them fall faster.

Afterimage

Friday's sun leans. The last shoppers hurry; a father buys pomegranates; a mother chooses fish. Candles catch and a table brightens; in another house a call slides across tile; in a third a bell rings once and again. Children wiggle; elders stand; someone stumbles over a prayer and smiles; someone else weeps without embarrassment. The week's seam is stitched. Above these roofs the same stars rise they've always risen; below them, the ground holds the footprints of others who kept time like this and argued like this and forgave like this. One God. Many paths. One neighborhood.

PART V: ESOTERIC MAPS & NEW AGE CURRENTS

CHAPTER 11

BODIES OF BREATH, CHAKRAS, CHANNELS, AND VITAL ENERGIES

At sunrise, a teacher asks her students to sit and notice a simple thing: breath touching the rim of the nose. "Follow it," she says, "down into the belly." The room quiets. Words for what they feel vary by culture and training, prāṇa, qi, rlung, àṣẹ, mana, but the intuition is shared: life moves in us like weather. Where it pools, paths, and tangles has long been mapped.

One family of maps among many

In Sanskrit, chakra means "wheel." In certain Tantric Hindu and Buddhist yogas, chakras are visualized as centers in a subtle body, linked by channels (nāḍī) through which vital breath (prāṇa, vāyu) is directed in meditation. These systems are plural, not fixed: different texts describe different numbers and locations of chakras (four, five, six, seven, eight, and more), with distinct deities, sounds, and petals. The image of a single, ancient, universal "seven-chakra" template is a modern simplification.

A landmark of the Sanskrit tradition for many modern readers is Sat-Cakra-Nirūpaṇa ("Description of the Six Centers"), a 16th-century Shakta–Tantric verse cycle later translated and popularized in English by Sir John Woodroffe (Arthur Avalon) in The Serpent Power (1919). These works describe lotuses at specific points along the central channel and practices to move kuṇḍalinī, a coiled, latent power, upward through them.

In Tibetan Vajrayāna, the subtle body is pictured with channels and winds (rlung), and chakra counts and placements again vary by lineage (completion-stage yogas of systems like Guhyasamāja, Hevajra, or Kālacakra). Here too, breath, visualization, and posture train attention to move through inner landscapes.

Across the Sinosphere, people speak of qi, psychophysical vitality, coursing through a network of meridians and pooling in dāntián (elixir fields), especially the lower field in the belly, center of breath and balance in martial and healing arts. Practice aims to cultivate, circulate, and harmonize this flow.

Other cultures name something similar in their own grammars. In Yorùbá thought, àṣẹ is the living power that makes things happen, present in persons, words, places, and rites, an aesthetic and ethical current as much as a "substance." In parts of Polynesia and Melanesia, mana names a potency that can adhere to people and objects and must be handled with care. These are not one-to-one with chakras or qi, but they rhyme in proposing that the world is animated, relational, and charged.

What these maps do for people

They teach attention (to breath, posture, sensation), ethics (conduct affects the flow of life), craft (methods for calm, focus, heat, stillness), and meaning (a story of how body and spirit interpenetrate). Whether one treats them as literal physiology, symbolic pedagogy, or both, practitioners use them to narrate change, to grieve, heal, choose, and hope.

How a modern "seven-chakra rainbow" arose

The familiar Western picture, seven chakras in a rainbow from tailbone to crown, linked with endocrine glands and modern psychology, doesn't come straight out of any single premodern text. It cohered through 19th–20th-century Theosophy and occult revival, notably with C. W. Leadbeater's illustrated The Chakras (1927), and then through late-20th-century teachers and authors (for example, Anodea Judith, Wheels of Life, first published in 1987). These works blended Indic sources with contemporary color theory, psychology, and Western esotericism; that's why studio posters today agree on colors that older Sanskrit sources do not. We present this as a reception history, a map with its own life and uses, distinct from classical Tantric manuals.

A small comparative walk

- South Asia, Tantric yogas. Varied chakra counts; breath retention, bandhas (locks), mantra, deity visualization; kuṇḍalinī rising as transformation.
- Tibet, winds and channels. Completion-stage yogas work with rlung in channels, often four or five primary centers, depending on tantra; aims include stability, bliss, and insight.
- China, qi, meridians, dāntián. Breath and movement (qigong, taiji) cultivate qi; lower dāntián (abdomen) is a hub for power and calm.
- Yorùbá, àṣẹ. A force in words, art, persons, and places; an ethic of character and relational power rather than an interior plumbing diagram.
- Oceania, mana. Potency that adheres to persons and objects; socially regulated and morally freighted. What science says (and doesn't)

Modern biomedicine does not recognize chakras, meridians, or mana as anatomical structures. Researchers do investigate adjacent phenomena, interoception (the brain's sensing of the body's internal state), autonomic regulation (breath and vagus-tone practices), and endogenous bioelectric signaling (how voltage gradients guide growth and repair). These lines of work describe physiology in their own terms and shouldn't be conflated with spiritual maps, though some people find them complementary. Reviews of "biofield" therapies show an active but heterogeneous research landscape with mixed quality and findings; claims of universal, measurable "subtle energy" remain contested. We'll keep distinctions clear while noting points of practical overlap (e.g., slow breathing improves mood and arousal regulation for many people, with or without a chakra frame).

How we know (notes from the toolkit)

- Texts, not one text. Sanskrit and Tibetan sources (tantras, manuals, commentaries) describe multiple chakra schemes; Roots of Yoga gathers key passages and shows their variety. English translations like Woodroffe's The Serpent Power shaped Western readings
- Terminology matters. "Chakra" (Indic), "qi/meridians/dāntián" (Sinosphere), "rlung/tsa" (Tibet), "àṣẹ" (Yorùbá), "mana" (Oceania) are family resemblances, not identities; we lean on regional scholarship rather than forcing equivalence.
- Reception history. The Theosophical movement and later New Age authors created today's standardized seven-center, rainbow-color picture; we cite their own publications to mark that pivot.
- Science in its lane. We reference peer-reviewed work on interoception and bioelectric signaling to explain current physiological frames, and transparent scoping reviews to show the state of "biofield" evidence.

Practice as story

Viewed as pedagogy, subtle-body maps train a reader to move attention through the interior like a pilgrim through shrines: root, belly, solar plexus, heart, throat, brow, crown, or another sequence, per lineage. Each station carries virtues and tests: steadiness and fear, appetite and generosity, warmth and courage, grief and love, truth and listening, pattern and insight, surrender and spaciousness. Whether or not one adopts the metaphysics, the narrative of ripening is clear, and many find it usable.

Ethics and care

Because these are living traditions, the book distinguishes between insider teachings and modern hybrids, credits lineages where appropriate, and respects limits around restricted instruction. We avoid medical claims and note that intense breath/visualization practices can destabilize some people; guidance matters.

Motif across worlds: Breath as Bridge

From Vedic hymns to monastic manuals, from Daoist treatises to Yorùbá praise poetry, breath stands between matter and meaning. It is both a measurable gas exchange and a metaphor for spirit, speech, and power. In nearly every tradition, to change the breath is to change the mind, and to speak well is to move the world.

Afterimage

The students rise. The room is ordinary again: mats, shoes at the door, a kettle clicking off. Outside, traffic thins and grows like a great lung. None of this proves a lotus in the spine. All of it proves that beings like us can be trained to attend, to soften, to steady, to speak carefully in a world that answers to words and deeds. That is reason enough for these maps to endure.

CHAPTER 12

THE SKY AS MIRROR

Astrology across cultures

Before dawn, a watcher climbs a stair. The city is sleeping; ovens are coals. He tilts a polished bowl, catches the star that should rise just ahead of the Sun, and marks a line on wax. Later, someone will read that mark beside a chart of births and a list of kings. Whether you call it omen, horoscope, or season, the human habit is the same: look up to understand down here.

Astrology begins with attention. People notice that certain lights wander among fixed stars; that some stars vanish into the Sun's glare and reappear; that eclipses repeat; that monsoons, Nile floods, and winds have rhythms. From attention grows a pattern, from a pattern a prediction, and from a prediction meaning. Different cultures teach the sky to speak in distinct grammars, but the impulse is shared: as above, so below, not as a law of physics in these pages, but as a language for living.

From omen lists to birth charts

In the first millennium BCE, scholars in Mesopotamia kept astronomical diaries and compiled long tables of omens: if a planet is in this sign and the Moon looks thus, a city prospers, or a king should beware. Over centuries, this public, state-centered sky talk has individualized. In Hellenistic Egypt, mathematicians and magicians synthesized Babylonian cycles, Egyptian decans (star clocks), and Greek geometry into the horoscope: a map cast for a moment (birth, a question, a coronation), using the ascending sign (the zodiac sign rising on the eastern horizon) to anchor a chart of houses that parcel out life's topics. That chart could be read for character and timing.

From there, traditions multiplied and traveled: via Greek and Demotic handbooks, through Syriac and Arabic scholars, into Persian and Latin compendia, and further still. The sky's mirror became portable.

How a chart talks (in a handful of lines)

A natal chart is a diagram of timing and angle, not a photograph of personality. It notes:

- **Where** the Sun, Moon, and planets stood against the **zodiac**, a belt of constellations turned into twelve equal signs (tropical in the West; **sidereal** in many Indian schools).
- **Which sign** was rising (the **Ascendant**), setting, culminating, and underground, anchors for the **houses**, each linked to areas of life (livelihood, kin, illness, travel, reputation, allies, the hidden).
- **Angles** (aspects) between planets, conjunction, square, trine, are treated as relationships or tensions.
- **Timelords** and cycles that "release" topics in sequence.

Astrologers then read the story this geometry suggests. Schools differ on details; everything depends on the tradition you inhabit and the questions you ask.

Lineages that learned different skies

Hellenistic & Greco-Roman. In the early centuries BCE/CE, manuals by astrologers such as Dorotheus, Vettius Valens, and Ptolemy set out techniques for natal, electional (choosing auspicious moments), mundane (cities and weather), and horary (questions) astrology. They fed a booming practice culture, physicians, magistrates, ship captains, and lovers all wanted the sky's counsel. Later, Byzantine and late antique readers preserved and argued these arts.

Arabic–Persian. Between the 8th and 12th centuries, scholars in Baghdad, Balkh, Rayy, and Córdoba translated and expanded Greek works, integrating them with Indian and Iranian materials. They refined astronomical tables, invented instruments (astrolabes), and wrote encyclopedias that influenced Europe for centuries. Astrology ran alongside medicine, geography, and optics in the same libraries.

India (Jyotiṣa). In South Asia, jyotiṣa ("the limb of light") evolved as a Vedic auxiliary discipline and, later, as a horoscopic art that both drew upon and diverged from Hellenistic methods. Most Indian schools use a sidereal zodiac anchored to star backgrounds, track the Moon through nakṣatras (27–28 lunar mansions), and time life with daśā periods (e.g., Vimśottarī), a distinctive system of unfolding "time-lords." The result is a rich, living tradition with its own logic, remedies, and ethics.

China & East Asia. Here, the sky speaks through the sexagenary cycle (ten heavenly stems × twelve earthly branches), the twelve-animal years, the twenty-eight lunar mansions, and systems such as the Four Pillars of Destiny (Bāzì) and Zǐwēi Dǒushù. Astrology braided with imperial astronomy, calendrics, medicine, and geomancy (fēngshuǐ); its aim was often civic and ethical order as much as individual fate.

Mesoamerica. Not astrology in the Greco-Egyptian mold, but a precise day-sign practice: the 260-day-tonalpohualli paired with a 365-day year made a Calendar Round; day signs and numbers shaped naming, divination, and rulership. Venus cycles mattered greatly; codices track its morning/evening apparitions with care.

Medieval & early modern Europe. Universities taught astronomy and astrology side by side; physicians cast charts; kings hired court astrologers; printers filled cities with almanacs. Critics flourished too; clergy and skeptics warned of excess or hubris. By the 17th century, the scientific revolution and changing tastes dimmed astrology's official standing, though it never vanished.

Modern revivals. The 19th–20th centuries saw occult and Theosophical currents reframe astrology; psychological astrology (Jung-inflected) recast fate as symbolic process; newspapers popularized Sun-sign columns; software made chart casting instant. Today, you'll find a spectrum, from traditionalists restoring old methods to innovators mixing astrology with therapy, art, or activism.

What the sky measures, and what people make of it

Astronomy measures motions: orbits, risings, eclipses, and precession (the slow wobble of Earth's axis that shifts star positions against seasons). Those motions explain why tropical Western astrology fixes Aries to the equinox, while many Indian schools keep a sidereal zodiac that drifts relative to seasons. Both are conventions with histories, not mistakes.

Astrology, by contrast, is an interpretive art. It claims that time has qualities, that moments "seed" patterns, and that the sky's cycles can correspond to life's rhythms. This book neither proves nor disproves those claims. It treats astrology as culture: a way communities have narrated character, chosen moments, and argued about ethics. It also notes the social work it does, holding anxiety, staging hope, giving language to uncertainty.

Ethics, remedies, and responsibility

Most living traditions warn against fatalism. A chart may counsel timing (when to begin or pause), remedies (charity, prayer, pilgrimage, mantra, ritual, offerings), and conduct (don't make a small flame into a house fire). Good practitioners, by their own codes, pair technique with care: do no harm; keep confidentiality; refuse predictions that strip people of agency.

A short walk among instruments and rooms

- An observatory roof. A scribe records the Moon's first crescent; below, merchants need the new month to open their books.
- A temple office. An astrologer lights a lamp, casts a chart, and discusses a couple's question about marriage, not as a verdict but as a conversation about timing and temperament.
- A court physician's bench. He checks a patient's pulse and a chart cast for the onset of fever; in his notebook, humors and constellations sit on the same page, whatever helps a body heal.
- A modern desk. Software draws a wheel in a blink; a client asks about career. The astrologer listens as much as she calculates; the chart becomes a mirror for dialogue.

How we know (notes from the toolkit)

- Tablets & papyri. Omen compendia, astronomical diaries, and personal horoscopes survive in clay and reed; they show the move from state omens to individual charts.
- Handbooks. Greek, Sanskrit, Arabic, Persian, and Latin manuals teach methods and carry debates; marginal notes reveal practitioners arguing with their teachers.
- Calendars & instruments. Astrolabes, water clocks, mural quadrants, nilometers, gnomons, and printed almanacs are the hardware of prediction.
- Crossings. Translation chains (Greek → Syriac/Arabic → Latin; Sanskrit ↔ Greek/Persian) leave fingerprints, loanwords, borrowed techniques, hybrid charts.
- Living lineages. Today's schools (traditional, Vedic, Chinese, psychological) teach and publish; their manuals and casebooks are primary sources for modern practice.

Cautions and boundaries

- Not medicine, not law. Historical astrology often touched these, but in this book it remains history and ethnography, not advice.
- Distinctions matter. Astronomy is measurement; astrology is interpretation. Mixing them without care confuses more than it clarifies.
- Cultural respect. We avoid collapsing jyotiṣa, Bāzì, and Hellenistic craft into one; each speaks its own language.
- Precession isn't a scandal. Systems choose different anchors; their value (for believers) lies in coherence and use, not in a single cosmic "true zodiac."

Motif across worlds: "As Above, So Below"

The phrase, polished by Hermetic texts, names less a law than a habit of mind: look for echoes between large and small, sky and street. It can mislead when turned into proof. It can instruct when kept as metaphor: remember scale; remember pattern; act with proportion.

Afterimage

Dawn burns the bowl of the sky. On a riverbank a farmer glances at the Moon and decides whether to flood a field; in an apartment a nurse checks her rota and a prayer app; in a small office a young man folds a printed chart and puts it in his pocket like a mirror. None of them need the stars to rise, the Sun will come regardless. And yet each has learned to time a life by rhythms larger than a mood. That may be astrology's most durable gift: a reminder that we live in company, with seasons, with cycles, with one another.

CHAPTER 13

NUMBERS WITH SOULS

Numerology across traditions

In a quiet room a teacher draws ten seeds from a bowl and lays them in a triangle: one, then two beneath, then three, then four. Ten from one and one from ten. She hums a note and slides a bridge along a string until the octave sings, the string now half its length. “Listen,” she says. “Proportion has a voice.” A child nods, not because she understands theorems, but because she hears that number can be more than count. It can be meaning.

This chapter follows that intuition across places and centuries. People everywhere have measured with numbers; many have also read with them, finding in certain counts and shapes a grammar for fate, character, or the hidden bonds between things. We keep two truths close: numbers are tools in nature’s laboratory, and they are also symbols in the human imagination. Confusing those truths breeds superstition; separating them too cleanly misses why numbers move us.

“All is number”: music, measure, and the oath of ten

In the Greek colonies of southern Italy, Pythagorean circles treated numbers not as mere tallies but as qualities. The tetraktys, 1+2+3+4, was a little mountain of seeds and an oath, the sum 10 standing for completeness. Intervals heard on a monochord, octave 2:1, fifth 3:2, fourth 4:3, made harmony feel like a ratio made sound. Even and odd wore temperaments; numbers could be male or female, square or oblong, perfect or deficient. A way of life grew around these ideas: plain food, shared property, study, song, and the belief that the soul could be tuned like a string.

Not all of this is mathematics as we practice it now. But it seeded a durable thought: proportion is beautiful, and beauty instructs. Architects, musicians, and theologians kept that lesson even when they let the oaths go.

When letters count: names, sums, and sacred arithmetic

Across the Mediterranean and Southwest Asia, alphabets also did duty as numerals. That doubled their storytelling power: words could carry numbers; numbers could echo words.

- In Hebrew traditions, gematria reads letters as values and notices meaningful sums. The custom of giving gifts in multiples of 18 (the value of ḥai, "life") is an example of arithmetic turned into ethics. Commentators sometimes pointed to the numerical kinship of words to prompt reflection, not to bind doctrine.
- In Greek circles, the practice is called isopsephy; a shared total suggested a kinship of ideas or an invitation to wordplay.
- In Arabic, the abjad order assigns numbers to letters; scribes, Sufis, and poets used these values to date inscriptions, ornament invocations, or meditate on divine names. At times and places, this grew into ʿilm al-ḥurūf, the "science of letters," where number, letter, and cosmology entwine.

This is not a single system but a family resemblance: letters are weights; names can be weighed.

Calendars that breathe numbers

Some numbers became the lungs of time.

- The week, seven days, braided heavenly lights and household rhythm.
- The year: twelve months will not fit neatly around the Sun's path; intercalations, nineteen-year cycles, and clever tables stitched lunations to seasons.

- In Mesoamerica, a 260-day count interlocked with a 365-day year; Venus cycles were tracked with exquisite care. Number here was navigation, not ornament.
- In China, the sexagenary cycle (ten heavenly stems × twelve earthly branches) paced years, months, days, and hours; diviners and administrators alike lived inside its hum.

To live by a calendar is to live inside an agreed number, a social covenant as much as a sky map.

China's pattern sense: squares, trigrams, and tones of luck

If numbers can be virtues, they can also be tones. In Chinese worlds, the Luòshū magic square of three, rows and columns summing to the same total, became a visual parable of balance. The Yìjīng's eight trigrams and sixty-four hexagrams turn broken and unbroken lines into a binary-like atlas of change: number as oracle of pattern. Everyday life keeps a lighter register: 8 as auspicious (a fortunate sound), 4 avoided in some places (a homophone for "death"), 9 long and imperial. Here, numerology blends with language play, architecture, and etiquette; it guides choices without claiming physics.

India's number-craft: counts, codes, and sacred totals

South Asian worlds braid rigorous mathematics with devotional counts. The navagraha (nine planetary powers) watch over rites; 108 beads slip through fingers in mantra, a total that harmonizes with other sacred counts (27 lunar mansions with four "quarters" each; 12 months × 9). Scholars turned syllables into numbers and back: the kaṭapayādi system let astronomers hide long constants in verses easy to memorize. Some later ankavidyā ("number knowledge") and modern "name-number" practices echo gematria and Pythagorean revival, but the older core is discipline and memory: numbers as ladders for prayer and science alike.

Africa's combinatorics of counsel

In Yorùbá Ifá, a diviner's palm-nuts or chain fall into one of 256 configurations, odu, each linked to a corpus of verses. This is not arithmetic in the Pythagorean sense nor gematria's letter-sums, but it is structure: 16 × 16 patterns form a matrix for story and advice. Number serves counsel the way a loom serves cloth: it holds the threads while meaning is woven.

Across the continent, proverbs turn counts into conduct: three for balance, four for the corners of community, seven or nine for completeness. These are not laws; they are rhythms that memory likes.

Christian number-sense: measure and mystery

Monastic handbooks and cathedral builders loved proportion, three as a figure of the Trinity, four as the earth's quarters, twelve as apostolic and civic, forty as trial and maturation. Augustine and others read numbers as a second scripture when used humbly, as vanity when used to bully texts into secrets. The Book of Revelation's "number of the beast" invited generations to puzzle and warn; the safest moral drawn was not arithmetical but ethical: beware of powers that demand worship.

Modern numerology: from parlor to poster

Between the late 19th and 20th centuries, occult revival and New Thought circles in Europe and North America blended Pythagorean lore, Kabbalistic hints, and popular psychology into what many readers know today as numerology: letters mapped to 1–9, names and birth dates reduced to "life path" digits, single-digit "virtues" assigned to people and years. Bestsellers and newspaper columns made it portable; later, New Age teachers kept it friendly and therapeutic.

This book treats modern numerology as reception history: a living map many people use to narrate change or seek counsel. It is not the same as ancient arithmetic or scripture's number sense, though it borrows elements from both.

What numbers do for us (besides count)

- They steady attention. A rosary's 59, a mala's 108, a tasbīḥ's 99 or 33, counts make prayer a habit you can feel.
- They compress meaning. An anniversary year, a jersey number, a doorway's address, digits carry identity in shorthand.
- They offer frames. "Seventh year," "nine-day novena," "forty days", numbers turn time into rooms where work can happen.
- They invite play. Riddles, magic squares, puzzles; the joy of a clean sum or a discovered pattern.
- They tempt excess. When a number is mistaken for fate, or a pattern spotted is treated as a decree, people can be boxed in by arithmetic that forgets mercy.

Boundaries and bridges with science

Modern science treats numbers as measurements and models. It does not find "vibrations" proper to the digit 7 in blood or stone. Yet science does confirm that humans are pattern-hungry: we learn better with repeatable units; we calm when breath is counted; we remember with rhythm. In that sense, some numerological practices act like behavioral tools even when their metaphysics are debated. The bridge we keep is used without overclaiming: let counting serve focus and community; let measurement serve truth.

A short gallery of numeric lives

- A craftsman's rule. In a timber yard, a worker lays out a staircase with a framing square etched with a table of risers and runs. The geometry on the tool is a public secret: a number turned into muscle memory.
- A scribe's margin. In a Hebrew book a reader tucks a tiny note: two words that share a value; a smile across centuries that says "look again."
- A shop sign in Guangzhou. The phone number features repeating eights; the rent was higher for it. A customer grins, it feels lucky to dial.
- A kitchen table. A bride and groom decide to give gifts in multiples of 18 for a cause they love. Arithmetic becomes alms.
- A small room at dawn. Fingers pass 108 beads; the breath evens; the day changes because the counter changed the watcher.

How we know (notes from the toolkit)

- Texts and testimonies. Pythagorean fragments and later reporters on their life; Jewish, Christian, and Muslim commentaries that use numbers with care; Chinese classics (Yìjīng, calendrical treatises) and manuals on magic squares; Sanskrit works on prosody and memory that encode numbers in verse; Ifá verse corpora organized by odu.
- Artifacts. Abaci, counting boards, astrolabes, monochords; talismans and amulets bearing letter-numbers; carved dates written as phrases whose value equals a year.
- Calendars and codes. Week structures, intercalation cycles, day-sign almanacs; letter-to-number schemes (gematria, isopsephy, abjad, kaṭapayādi) used in dated inscriptions and scientific verse.
- Reception trails. 19th–20th-century occult and New Thought publications that systematize "name numbers" and popularize

life-path schemes; newspapers and handbooks that standardize charts we now treat as "classic."

We distinguish historical uses (anchored to sources and institutions) from modern hybrids (anchored to teachers and communities of practice). Both belong here; they do different work.

Motif across worlds: Ten, Twelve, and the One More

So many human sets come in ten, twelve, and thirteen. Ten rides the hands; twelve rides moons and markets (dozens, hours); thirteen asks to be added, lunar to solar, household to council, friend to circle. Cultures teach which totals feel complete and which feel excess. The motif is more than quaint: it's how communities agree on enough, enough judges, enough months, enough steps to the shrine.

Afterimage

Night falls on a city that still runs by numbers: bus schedules, oven temperatures, hymn numbers slotted into a wooden rack, cricket scores, street addresses climbing by twos. In an upstairs room, a teenager traces her name through a chart from the internet and laughs at how perfectly and imperfectly it fits. In a downstairs kitchen, a grandfather counts out pills and then, without thinking, counts the fourteen breaths he learned long ago before lifting a fork. In a bookbinder's shop, a small magic square decorates a cover in gold, playful, precise. Numbers have done what stories ask of them: they have remembered us to ourselves.

CHAPTER 14

CARDS THAT LEARNED TO SPEAK

Tarot's journey from game to divination

On a linen cloth a reader shuffles, cuts, and turns three cards. A crowned woman holds a sword upright; a figure balances two pentacles in an infinity loop; a fool steps toward the edge, a small dog leaping at his heel. The room is ordinary, tea, a draft at the window, yet the pictures feel like a stage set for a conversation the sitter was already having with themself. That is tarot's quiet trick: pictures that invite speech.

A game before an oracle

Tarot began as play. In 15th-century northern Italy, courtly decks, painted gold and bright, later printed for townsfolk, added a parade of triumphs (trumps) to the familiar four suits. Players called the game tarocchi; the trumps, Fool, Empress, Emperor, Lovers, Chariot, Justice, Hermit, Fortune's Wheel, Death, Judgment, and the rest, were point-scoring images and moral theater, not secret doctrine. Early decks vary, no single canon, because they were made to be used.

Over time, standardized patterns spread, notably the Marseille style in French-speaking lands. The pack's structurestabilized around 78 cards: 22 trumps (later the "major arcana") and 56 suit cards (later the "minor"), four suits of ten pips plus court cards. For centuries, people mostly shuffled, played, and wagered.

How pictures learned to talk

In the late 18th century, antiquarian imaginations recast tarot as an ancient book without words. Writers in Paris proposed Egyptian origins, correspondences with Hebrew letters and astrology, and methods for cartomancy (divination with cards). A century later, occult and magical revivals layered further correspondences; by the early 20th century, new illustrated decks, most famously the Rider–Waite–Smith (1909), drawn by Pamela Colman Smith to the guidance of A. E. Waite, and later the Thoth deck painted by Frieda Harris with Aleister Crowley, made the pip cards themselves miniature scenes. Now every card "spoke" even to a beginner.

In the late 20th and 21st centuries, tarot globalized. Indie artists redrew archetypes through many lenses, feminist, Indigenous, diasporic, queer, ecological, so that more readers could see their lives in the cards. You can still play the original trick-taking games in Europe; you can also find therapists using decks as projective tools for storytelling and reflection (not as diagnosis).

What a reading really is

A reading is a structured conversation with pictures and chance.

- The draw. Randomness keeps the reader honest; it prevents stacking the deck with what the sitter already expects.
- The spread. Positions give grammar, past/present/future; the situation/the obstacle/the resource; the seen/the unseen/the way through.
- The image. Each card is an allegory: not a fixed fate but a tension to consider. A woman with a lion's jaw under her hand suggests that courage can be gentle; a tower struck by fire says sudden truth can feel like loss and still be liberation.
- The dialogue. Good readers ask: What do you see? Where does this hit? What would "the Hermit" mean if it were wise solitude rather than escape?

Seen this way, tarot is less about foretelling than framing, helping a person name what they already know and choose a next step more cleanly.

The deck as a portable theater

- The Majors (0–21) feel like a journey: innocence, choice, will, law, turning, crisis, vision, and return. Not every life plays all acts, but the sequence makes a myth of growth that many find illuminating.
- The Minors ground the myth: Wands for energy and enterprise, Cups for feeling and relation, Swords for thought and conflict, Pentacles for body and work, four ways a day can go right or wrong. The numbered cards show escalation; the courts mirror social roles and temperaments.

Cross-threads: number, star, letter

Tarot's later history is a mesh of correspondences, to numerology (one seeds, ten culminates), to astrology (cards linked to planets, signs, decans), and to letter-mysticism (paths on the Tree of Life). These links are modern stitch-work, not original to the game. They matter because they help practitioners hold a coherent symbolic language, useful, as long as we remember when the sewing happened.

Ethics, boundaries, care

- Consent and scope. A reading is by invitation; it is not a license to diagnose illness, predict death, or trespass on another's privacy.
- Agency. Cards are mirrors, not masters. A reader can name dynamics and timing without stealing choice.
- Humility. "I don't know" belongs in the room; so does "this might be wrong."
- Context. In many countries fortune-telling laws exist because of historic exploitation; responsible practice keeps money, power, and care in view.

How we know (notes from the toolkit)

- Objects. Museum-held early decks (e.g., aristocratic hand-painted cards; later woodcuts) show tarot's game origins and varied imagery.
- Printed rules & manuals. Early rulebooks teach play; 18th–20th-century treatises teach divination and layer correspondences.
- Reception trails. Diaries, shop records, advertisements, and court cases trace how cards moved from salons to street corners to bookstores to therapy offices.
- Living practice. Contemporary readers publish casebooks and codes of ethics; artists' notes reveal intent behind new decks.

Motif across worlds: Casting Lots, Casting Light

From drawing straws to throwing bones, from Ifá's odu to cleromancy in sacred texts, cultures use chance to cut through stuckness. The logic is not magic but disruption: let randomness loosen the grip of a rehearsed story, then reflect. Tarot stands in that lineage, lots that invite light.

Afterimage

The reader gathers the cards, squares the deck, and breathes. The sitter folds the note they made: one question, two options, three small actions to try. Outside the window, a bus hisses by; somewhere a child practices scales; upstairs, a neighbor makes tea. The pictures go back into the box; the conversation goes on in the sitter's head, which is the point. The cards returned what they were asked for: not certainty, but company.

CHAPTER 15

THE HAND'S MAP

Palmistry and the stories bodies tell

A woman holds out her palm across a café table. A reader tilts it to the light, notices the way fingers set from the knuckles, the soft square of the palm, the depth of a line that curves toward the thumb. "You hold on hard," the reader says, "and you're learning to loosen." The woman laughs; her right hand has calluses from tools; the line the reader named is a scar from a bottle that broke twenty years ago. The hand tells two stories at once: what life has done, and what the reader sees.

Many paths to the same palm

Reading the hand, chiromancy, has walked many roads. Texts in South Asia collected under samudrika śāstra (the lore of bodily signs) listed auspicious and inauspicious marks, including on hands and feet. Greek and Roman writers combined chiromancy with physiognomy; medieval and early modern Europe copied hand diagrams in manuscripts and printed manuals; Arabic and Persian treatises accompanied physicians and astrologers. In the 19th-century occult revival, palmistry joined tarot and numerology in parlors and pamphlets; laws against fortune-telling chased it into fairs and private rooms; it never left kitchens and barracks, where people still traced lines for jokes and comfort.

There is no single orthodoxy. Schemes differ on the names and meanings of mounts, lines, and finger types. What endures is the impulse: the body as a readable text.

What readers look at

- Shape & proportion. Long fingers, square palm; short fingers, long palm; the spread between thumb and index; the set of the little finger; the flex of joints. These are read as temperaments: fast/slow, concrete/abstract, reserved/expressive.
- Mounts. Cushions at the palm's base, named after planets in some systems (Venus below the thumb, Moon on the outer palm, etc.), are read for emphasis: appetite, imagination, drive, steadiness.
- Lines. Common names are life, head, heart, fate, Apollo, each read for quality (deep/light, broken/clear), path, and intersections. Scars and work marks complicate the tale, which is part of the charm: the hand records events.
- Skin & prints. Dermatoglyphics, arches, loops, whorls, are modern tools for identity and genetics; palmists long before noticed their variety and made symbolic use of it.

A responsible reader treats these features as prompts, not verdicts: ways to talk about stress and rest, attachment and solitude, attention and distraction, risk and patience.

Why hands invite belief

Hands are public and personal. They lift, hold, soothe, strike, make; they show age and work; they carry family resemblances and accidents. To look closely at a hand is to pay someone an unusual kind of attention, an intimacy that can be healing or exploitative depending on care. A palm reading, like a tarot session, is often a counsel hour disguised as a curiosity.

Where metaphor meets physiology

Modern biomedicine does not endorse palm lines as fate markers. Yet it does find meaningful links between the body and life: stress shows in nails and skin; hormones shape fat pads and joint laxity; repetitive work writes calluses and causes tendon thickening; connective-tissue conditions and genetics can influence line appearance. In that sense, the hand is, literally, a journal, but one best read for history, not destiny.

Ethics and limits

- No diagnoses. A reader is not a clinician; if a mole worries you, see a doctor.
- Consent and context. Palm readings should be invited; no grabbing strangers' hands, no "reading" someone to win an argument.
- Agency. "You have a stubborn streak" is a description; "you will die at 53" is a harm. Good readers avoid doom and keep choice in view.
- Cultural respect. Some lineages (e.g., elements of samudrika śāstra) carry religious and social weight; handle with care, cite sources, note what is restricted.

How we know (notes from the toolkit)

- Texts & images. Sanskrit compendia of bodily marks; Greco-Roman and Arabic treatises that mix chiromancy with physiognomy; medieval diagrams of hands labeled with stars and virtues; 19th-century handbooks that standardize "modern" palmistry.
- Law & reception. Ordinances against fortune-telling; court cases; pamphlets and posters advertising readers; memoirs and interviews with practitioners.
- Bodies as archives. Comparative studies of work marks, skinfolds, and dermal patterns are useful to explain why hands look as they do, independent of omen.

Motif across worlds: The Body as Book

From tattoo to scarification, from monastic tonsure to braided hair, from posture in prayer to athletic stance, humans turn bodies into texts. Palmistry sits in that broad family, a way of saying that character is written and also rewritten by habit and care. Even if you never read a line, your palms will tell: hammer or harp, hoe or keyboard, child lifted or grief clenched.

Afterimage

The reader releases the hand. The woman rubs her palm, amused and a little moved. She walks home thinking about the grip she uses on problems, too tight, maybe, and about the bottle scar and the night it came from. She takes a slower breath, flexes her fingers, and sets water to boil. On the counter, her hands look the way they always did, but she sees work and weather in them now. The map didn't foretell; it reminded.

CHAPTER 16

SHASTA, A MOUNTAIN OF MANY MEANINGS

At first light the mountain is a quiet instruction. Snow flares; the lava cone throws a long blue shadow over forests that still remember fire. Below the treeline, springs thread through meadows where wildflowers lift their faces even in lean summers. People come here to breathe, to pray, to ask. Long before road signs, the Winnemem Wintu and neighboring peoples came for ceremony and water; they still do. They ask visitors to tread like guests: step softly at Panther Meadows, do not carry away what does not belong to you, remember that sacredness is not a view but a relationship.

The older story: homeland, ceremony, obligation

For Indigenous communities of the region, Shasta is kin. Places have names, and names carry duties, how to gather, when to leave a meadow to rest, which springs to approach with care, where to sing and where to be silent. Story and practice run together: a mountain's spirit is not a metaphor; it is a neighbor. Ceremonies, some public, some restricted, keep that relation in balance. Elders remind newcomers that a "trail" is not just a path but a line of teaching: who went before, which plants offered themselves there, which harms were done, which are still being mended.

Modern pressures walk up the ridge with hikers: traffic, trash, drone buzz, social-media geotags that pull crowds to fragile places. Down-slope, policy battles over water and land, reservoirs, salmon runs, forest burns, reach into the mountain's stories. The local lesson is not abstract: respect is practical, and ceremony without stewardship rings hollow.

A new layer: Lemurians in the snow

In 1905, a novel appeared in California with a long afterlife: A Dweller on Two Planets. It told of a hidden city beneath Shasta, built by survivors of Lemuria, a lost continent imagined by earlier writers to explain certain fossils and peoples' distributions before plate tectonics did that better. The book's halls and tunnels, its sages and machines, turned the mountain into a door to elsewhere. Readers passed the story hand to hand; it stuck to the place the way burrs stick to a wool coat.

In the 1930s, a prospector named Guy Ballard said he met an Ascended Master, Saint Germain, on the mountain. He and his wife Edna launched the "I AM" Activity, preaching individual spiritual uplift through decrees, violet flames, and a chain of masters. Publications, lectures, and rallies made Shasta a magnet for those seeking modern revelation. Later metaphysical currents, Theosophy's wide net, New Thought's optimism, UFO lore, braided their threads through the same ridge.

Today, town and mountain show the layers plainly. You can buy crystals and a sandwich on the same block. Weekend gatherings promise meditations, vortex tours, or channeled teachings. The line between tourist economy and spiritual seeking is blurry; most people are earnest, some are careless; the mountain is patient and not infinite.

Stone and snow: the ground's own story

Shasta is a stratovolcano in the Cascade Range, a pile of eruptions stacked over hundreds of thousands of years. Glaciers still comb its flanks in small bright tongues. Springs rise where snowmelt threads through fractured rock. The cone's symmetry tricks the eye into timelessness, but the mountain is young by geologic standards and alive. Its hazards, ash, lahars, and fast snowmelt belong to a working earth. Fire chalks the lower forests; lightning argues the crown.

Geology is not at odds with sacredness; it is one of the mountain's voices.

Layers, not replacements

The mountain's modern metaphysical stories do not erase its older sacredness. They sit on top of it, sometimes in harmony, sometimes in friction. A respectful visitor can notice three layers and keep the boundaries clear:

- Indigenous Shasta, living relationships, protocols, and ceremonies that predate and outlast every settler story.
- Geologic Shasta, a volcano with its own clocks, feeding springs, and soils, and teaching constraint.
- Metaphysical Shasta, a 20th-century and ongoing flowering of teachings about hidden cities, ascended masters, vortices, and personal transformation.

The risk is not plurality. The risk is confusion, treating a meadow open to all as if it were an altar without asking, or treating a ceremony that asks for privacy as if it were a backdrop for content. The cure is simple and hard: learn local guidance, ask, and accept "no."

Three scenes on one day

- At Panther Meadows. A family arrives at dawn, leaves offerings of water, and sings softly. On a small sign nearby, a request: stay on the path; the meadow heals slowly from footsteps. One child leans toward the spring as if to hear it better.
- In town at noon. A group in white carries singing bowls into a park; a veteran hiker with scratched calves shows a newcomer how to pack out orange peels because the elevation keeps them from rotting quickly. Across the street, a shopkeeper sets out a "be kind to the mountain" jar for local stewardship.

- On the ridge at dusk. A climber ties in, checks a friend's knot, and points at a gray ribbon on the slope. "Old lahar," she says. "If the mountain runs, it runs fast. Watch the weather."

What Shasta tells this book

Mountains collect stories because they collect weather and time. Shasta reminds us that sacred geographies are plural: a place can be home, teacher, hazard, altar, and business district at once. It also reminds us that meanings have authors: the Winnemem Wintu's meanings arise from kinship and promise; the novel's meanings arise from a printing press; a shop's meanings arise at a register. Putting them in one chapter is not to flatten them. It is to practice reading with labels on.

How we know (notes from the toolkit)

- Tribal testimony & local guidance. Public statements from the Winnemem Wintu and other Native communities; field notes and oral histories; requests posted at meadows and springs.
- Printed sources. Early editions of A Dweller on Two Planets, "I AM" Activity pamphlets and lectures, and later New Age publications and town archives.
- Geology & ecology. USGS maps, volcanic hazard assessments, glacier surveys, and spring studies; forest management records; fire histories.
- Ethics & policy. Land management plans; closures; court records where sacred access intersects with public rules.

Motif across worlds: The Mountain That Teaches

From Sinai to Kailash, Fuji to Uluru, mountains are teachers: they hold weather, hide water, demand breath, and compel proportion. People climb them for instruction, some return with tablets or vows, some with quiet. The motif's danger is conquest dressed as pilgrimage. Its gift is humility: altitude as an argument for listening.

Afterimage

Night winds draw cold down the gullies. Headlamps bob like slow comets up a snowfield; lower, crickets try their late-summer hymn. In town, a shopkeeper flips a sign to CLOSED; a camper folds a tarp before the dew sets; a grandmother tells a story to a child that ends with "and this is why we do not step there." The mountain is not a blank screen for our wishes. It is an older neighbor with weather and work and its own long ways of speaking. If we learn to hear them, we might become better neighbors ourselves.

CHAPTER 17

UNDERWORLDS & UNDERGROUNDS, CAVES TO ANTARCTICA

Sometimes the world continues downward. In the soft volcanic tuff of Cappadocia, doorways open in the ground and lead to rooms, galleries, stables, chapels, and long sloping corridors. Derinkuyu drops like a spiral well, level after level, enough space for thousands. The air moves through shafts; stone doors roll on hidden pivots to seal a passage; soot clocks the ceilings. It is not legend. It is architecture made of fear and foresight and patience.

Underground, by necessity and by craft

Humans go below for many reasons: refuge from raiders, shelter from heat, storage against spoilage, prayer in quiet, the thrill or dread of descent.

- Cappadocia (Anatolia). Towns honeycombed underground cities from old cellars, enlarging them under pressure, Hittite times, Byzantine times, Seljuk times, opening and closing entrances as danger ebbed and flowed. Frescoes survive in ground-level rock-cut churches; deeper rooms carry only tool marks and smoke.
- Coober Pedy (Australia). In a baked landscape, people live in dugouts that hold steady temperatures; hotels, churches, and homes tuck into sandstone. Architecture adapts: light wells, careful drainage, shared corridors.
- Cellars, caves, cisterns. From Mediterranean cisterns and wine caves to North African qanat galleries and monastic cells cut into cliff, underground space extends above-ground life: cool storage, hidden water, a room for repeated prayer.

Going below is not just escape. It is a design choice: how to borrow earth's insulation, how to make a wall from what you would otherwise walk on.

Underworlds of story

Long before and alongside practical burrows, people mapped moral and cosmic worlds beneath:

- Mesoamerica. The Popol Vuh's Xibalba is a place of trials, dark houses, bat houses, blade houses, where wit and courage are tested before renewal. Cenotes (water-filled sinkholes) and caves were entrances, thresholds where offerings traveled.
- Greece. Hades is not only punishment; it is a gray ordinary where shades drink memory and heroes bargain. Orpheus turns back; Odysseus consults. The underworld is a council chamber for limits.
- The Southwest. Hopi stories speak of emergence from earlier worlds through a sipapuni, a small earth navel; the place that opens is both exit and promise, a reminder that the present world requires balance to endure.
- Mesopotamia. Kur is a land of no return where the dead eat dust; Inanna's descent and return teaches rule and restraint.
- Others: Maori descent into Rarohenga, Norse Hel, Polynesian journeying to ancestral islands, African rivers you cross with a coin or a phrase, each with its own grammar for how to live above.

Underworld travel frames ethics: keep vows; mind your speech; repay debts; honor the dead; don't mistake power for permission.

Modern esoteric geographies

In the late 19th century, European occult imaginations abstracted and systematized old motifs. Agartha (or Agharta) entered print as a hidden inner kingdom under deserts and mountains, later blending with Theosophical Shambhala (a Tibetan Buddhist idea reshaped in translation). "Hollow Earth" tales, polar openings, inner suns, subterranean races, skittered around pamphlets and pulp. In the 20th century, some of these stories relocated to specific maps: the Himalaya, the Amazon, and, especially, Antarctica. In this book, we treat these as modern myths: revealing of longings (refuge, wisdom, reset), alive in communities, distinct from geology.

Antarctica: the real underworld of ice

Beneath Antarctica's miles-thick ice lie subglacial lakes and rivers. Lake Vostok is a giant, sealed for hundreds of thousands of years, dark and pressurized; smaller lakes and channels stream under the ice sheet, where pressure and geothermal heat keep them liquid. Scientists read these waters and the ice above them like time capsules, microbes that teach survival, gases that archive ancient air, dust that records wind.

Further south still, under the Amundsen–Scott Station at the Pole, the IceCube Neutrino Observatory strings thousands of sensors deep in clear ice to catch faint blue flashes when particles from distant supernovae or black holes interact. The South Pole is quiet enough, cold enough, and dark enough to make the Earth itself a lens.

Ice cores pulled from the plateau show annual layers like tree rings. Trapped bubbles carry ancient atmosphere; ratios of oxygen isotopes track temperature. In those narrow cylinders, under a fluorescent lab light, researchers see the long breathing of the planet, glacial advances and retreats, volcanic winters, slow rises, and sudden spikes.

About those "Antarctic pyramids" and secret cities

Photos of sharp-shouldered peaks on the ice sometimes ricochet around the internet with captions about pyramids. The geology is plainer and stranger: nunataks, rock summits that poke through ice, shaped by frost and wind. Their pyramid looks are coincidence and erosion; the ice hides no ancient masonry at its base. Similar legends pulse about secret bases and hidden civilizations under the ice. In this book, there are topics, not timelines, useful for understanding the urge to relocate paradise or the threat to a hard-to-reach map edge.

How we know (notes from the toolkit)

- Archaeology of the underground. Plans of Cappadocian sites; tool marks and soot; carbon dates from organic remains; reused spaces that track centuries of need.
- Ethnography & oral traditions. Recorded tellings (with permissions) and living practice around caves, cenotes, and emergence places; protocols for entry; maps of taboo.
- Geophysics & glaciology. Radar and seismic surveys that image subglacial topography and lakes; GPS stations that track ice flow; chemical and biological assays from carefully sampled waters and ice.
- Particle physics in ice. Detector arrays, calibration runs, and sky maps from neutrino observatories; public data that show how a deep, cold medium becomes a telescope.
- Media archaeology. The chain of pamphlets, novels, and radio shows that took "Hollow Earth" from metaphor to subgenre.

Why we keep going down

Descent is a shape of thought. We go down to fetch water, salt, coolness, safety, memory, counsel, and to learn limits. You cannot swagger in a narrow passage; you must bend. The underground teaches proportion.

Three descents

- A ladder in a shaft. Your hands ring metal. You drop into a cool room where a lampshelf has held flame for lifetimes. Someone once slept here with a hundred others, listening to boots on the ground above.
- A cenote at noon. The sun is a coin in a blue throat. A keeper asks for quiet, and the water answers with a single drop from a root. Offerings glitter in the silt where light cannot quite touch them.
- A lab at midnight. A graduate student leans against a humming freezer and watches a monitor that marks the arrival of a single neutrino traced back to a galaxy she will never see. She smiles and makes tea. Somewhere, a katabatic wind carves snow into knives.

Motif across worlds: Descent for Return

Myths of descent end not in staying, but in returning with something: a law, a name, a seed, a warning, a song. Practical descents do too: water in a skin, mushrooms in a basket, a cooler house, a plan. The pattern teaches that depth is not a home by itself; it is a school.

Afterimage

Morning fills the shaft at Derinkuyu; a guide checks a gate and hums. In Mexico, a diver coils a rope beside a cenote and thanks a guardian under her breath. In Antarctica, a meteorologist reads a drum chart of wind and compares it to one from forty years ago. On a message board, someone posts a fresh photo of a sharp-lined nunatak and asks, "Pyramid?" In a classroom, a child draws a triangle and then a cave and then, without quite knowing why, a ladder between them. Above and below, the same lesson repeats: the earth keeps rooms for us if we learn the key.

PART VI: WORLDS IN MOTION

CHAPTER 18

OCEANS AS HIGHWAYS

Between May and October, the wind blows one way; between November and April, it turns and blows the other. Merchants on the Indian Ocean write their diaries in monsoon: load pepper when the southwest wind begins, pay the porter who knows the sandbar's mood, pray at the harbor shrine, and raise a lateen sail into a clock you can feel on your face. Oceans are not empty space; they are roads with seasons.

The first blue water

Long before bronze bells rang in ports, people learned the grammar of coast and current. In Southeast Asia, sailors lashed outriggers to canoes to steady a narrow hull; from those experiments came double-hulled voyaging canoes, able to carry people, animals, crops, and stories across Oceania. Navigators learned stars by rising and setting points, counted swells with their bodies, watched cloud color over unseen atolls, and followed birds at dawn and dusk. They built stick charts that taught how islands bend wave patterns. Pottery with shared designs (Lapita) and the travels of plants and animals trace a widening arc from Near Oceania into Remote Oceania, Fiji, Tonga, Samoa, then onward, centuries later, to Hawai‘i, Aotearoa, and Rapa Nui. The ocean became a map you memorize, then sing.

Far to the west, toward Africa, other blue-water feats unfolded. Southeast Asian sailors reached Madagascar in antiquity, their language becoming Malagasy, their boat forms and crops joining African ones; on the Swahili coast, stone towns faced the sea with coral rag walls, mosques, and warehouses, talking in a Bantu tongue salted with Persian and Arabic words. Oceans knit diasporas long before the word existed.

The Indian Ocean world

Imagine a loop: East Africa, Arabia, Persian Gulf, Gujarat, Malabar, Sri Lanka, Coromandel, Bay of Bengal, Sumatra, Java, Malacca, South China Sea, and back by the opposite wind. On this loop sailed dhows with lateen triangles and junks with stiff, battened sails; aboard: pepper, cloves, cinnamon, cardamom; cottons and silks; iron tools; porcelain; beads and cowries; ambergris and ivory; dates and rice. With the cargo traveled people and prayers: Muslims, Hindus, Buddhists, Jains, Jews, and later Christians worked the same wharves and often lodged in the same neighborhoods.

Ports were entrepôts, not empires, places like Kilwa, Aden, Hormuz, Calicut, Quilon, Malacca, ruled by sultans, shahs, rajas, or councils who taxed lightly enough to keep ships returning. Trust traveled by letters of credit and reputation; a merchant's word chained across cousins and partners from Zanzibar to Cambay to Palembang. Law was plural: qāḍī courts for some, guild rules for others, temple endowments for many; a contract might be witnessed by a monk and a mufti on the same bench.

When Islam spread along these coasts, it did so trader by trader, marriage by marriage; mosques rose beside shrines already old. Conversion was often as much civic as theological: a way to share law, credit, and companionship across waters. Elsewhere, Buddhist monasteries served as caravansaries of learning and storage; Hindu temples owned land and funded ships; Chinese tribute missions and private junk fleets braided the South China Sea into the same cloth.

The Mediterranean: a smaller, crowded sea

The Mediterranean is a bowl with many spoons. Phoenician sailors hugged coasts and planted colonies that became heirs, Carthage among them. Greek merchants and colonists cast island-hopping nets; Rome made the sea a logistics engine (mare nostrum) that fed cities with grain, oil, and wine shipped in amphorae stacked like beehives in hulls. After Rome's fall, Byzantine, Arab, and Italian mariners argued and traded over the same straits. A change in sail, lateentriangles, let ships tack more nimbly; a change in paperwork, commenda partnerships, let strangers risk together. The Mediterranean taught the world the arts of short hops, hard bargains, and fast news.

North Atlantic edges

Norse sailors pushed their clinker-built boats along the North Atlantic's stepping-stones, Shetland, the Faroes, Iceland, Greenland, and briefly Vinland in North America. They navigated with sun, birds, currents, and memory, cycling hay and stock across sea meadows as if fjords had grown long. Later, other Atlantic experiments would redraw maps; here, we mark that even cold seas grow roads where coasts consent.

South China Sea and beyond

Chinese mariners refined the compass, the sternpost rudder, and watertight bulkheads; junk rigs spread sail power across panels you could reef in storms. In the early 1400s, Zheng He's fleets, multi-masted behemoths escorted by smaller ships, sailed to Southeast Asia, India, Arabia, and East Africa, projecting courtly power, trading, and collecting tributary emissaries. The voyages did not found colonies; they announced presence. When court priorities turned inland, these sea roads did not vanish; private and regional shipping carried on, stitching Fujian, Guangdong, Champa, Java, and Luzon into family networks that survived dynasties.

Technologies that tamed distance (and never entirely)

- Hulls & rigs. Outrigger, double hull, sewn plank, carvel and clinker planking, lateen and crab-claw sails, junk panels, each a compromise with wind and wave.

- Steering & sighting. Tiller and axial rudders, sternposts, quarter-rudders; astrolabes and later cross-staffs; the magnetic compass; lead lines for depth; a hand in the water for temperature and current.
- Knowledge of bodies. Star compasses memorized as songs; the etak method in Micronesia (imagining the canoe still and islands moving past); pilots' books filled with soundings, capes, and tricks known only after a dozen tries.
- Trust & paper. Hawala and suftaja (credit), notarized contracts, seals, warehouses that doubled as temples or mosques, guilds to arbitrate and avenge.

Cargoes that change cookfires and calendars

Oceans carry tastes. Bananas and taro cross into Africa; rice varieties travel both ways; coconuts and breadfruit leap islands; spices reset cuisines across continents. Porcelain remakes table manners from Cairo to Kilwa; cottons from Gujarat recolor wardrobes in Southeast Asia; East African ivory becomes Chinese brush handles; iron from India becomes African tools; along many coasts, enslaved people are taken as cargo by neighbors long before Atlantic slavers arrive, reminding us that seas can traffic both gifts and grief.

Some cargoes travel as hitchhikers: rats, weeds, insects, and diseases change ecologies; ideas do, too; scripts, saints, stories, and gods learn new languages at the tide line.

Ports as schools of pluralism

Well-run ports are compromised machines. They teach people to bargain with accent and ritual, to share neighborhoods and wells, to keep holy days without breaking harbor days. They also raise hard questions about power: who sets the tax, patrols the water, and decides who may anchor? Where cities balanced these well, they grew rich and strange in the best sense; where they failed, pirates and empires filled the gap.

How we know (notes from the toolkit)

- Wrecks & harbors. Shipwreck cargoes, amphorae, ingots, ceramics, map routes; anchors and piers record forgotten shorelines; harbor mud traps pollen, seeds, and trash that tell who came and what they carried.
- Languages & lineages. Loanwords for boat parts and spices; place-names; the Malagasy language's Southeast Asian roots; DNA of commensal animals (like rats and chickens) that track human paths.
- Oral charts & chants. Navigators' teaching songs, stick charts, and voyaging genealogies, living archives of course and current.
- Pilots' books & itineraries. Sailing directions and merchants' handbooks; travelers' journals; court records of maritime lawsuits; inscriptions naming donors in dockside shrines and mosques.
- Plants & potsherds. Crops and their ancient DNA; Lapita sherds with distinctive stamps; beads in burials far from their source.

Motif across worlds: The Wind That Returns

Monsoon, trade wind, land breeze, sea breeze, the wind is a promise that comes back. People everywhere ritualize its return: launch days, first-fruits for the harbor god, the painter who mends the hull in the lull. The motif's lesson is practical and moral: plan for the season, not the day; know when to wait; know when to go together.

Three horizons

- An atoll before dawn. A navigator kneels in the sand and draws a star path with a stick. A boy watches and repeats the names under his breath; a woman loads breadfruit and pigs. The canoe will not follow the drawing; the crew will.

- Calicut at noon. The market smells of pepper and ghee. A Gujarati broker jokes with a Yemeni sailor over weights; a scribe copies a contract twice; a temple cook buys rice with a copper coin that yesterday was a pearl-seller's prayer.
- Malacca at dusk. Tide turns; a junk's shadow crosses a dhow; the harbor master's drum thumps a curfew; kettles hiss along the quay; someone sings a hymn in a language learned two monsoons ago and already home.

Afterimage

Night folds over the roadstead. Anchors creak; a watchman coughs; phosphorescence writes green on the bow of a skiff. On shore, street dogs settle by the fish market. Far out, a white line of surf mutters over a sandbar that ate a careless pilot last year. Tomorrow, if the wind keeps its promise, sails will flower again and the road will move without leaving a track. Oceans keep our oldest highways not in stone but in memory and weather, and we keep them by teaching both.

CHAPTER 19

EMPIRES & EDGES

A rider changes horses without dismounting. The new gelding surges; a leather tube thumps against the rider's ribs, dispatches sealed with clay, all speed and dust. At the next post house, a clerk stamps the time on a sliver of wood; a cook slides a bowl across the counter; a stable boy grins at the coins. This is an empire felt not as edict but as road, posts, fodder, measures, names. Somewhere, a governor is waiting for news; somewhere, a village hopes the news is not about more men demanded for a canal. Empires knit distance. Edges test the seams.

The grammar of big power

Empires are stories told in infrastructure. They put rules into roads, weights, walls, calendars, coins, canals, censuses, granaries, garrisons, and the classroom. They standardize just enough to tax and recruit; they promise order, courts, and grain in return. They do not last by force alone. They cultivate habits of speech (a lingua franca), of time (an official new year), of measure (the cubit here equals the cubit there), of loyalty (oaths, stipends, honors). When they succeed, strangers can bargain without drawing knives. When they fail, roads carry rebels as quickly as tax grain.

Centers and corridors

- Between the rivers to the sea. The Achaemenid kings ruled from Susa, Persepolis, and Babylon by sending orders down a Royal Road that ran like a backbone through satrapies (provinces). Aramaic greased commerce; local gods and elites found places in a wide frame. Later Hellenistic kingdoms, then Parthian and Sasanian courts, kept corridors alive between plateau, steppe, and Mediterranean, archers for hire, silk caravans under escort, embassies with gifts and grammar books.

- Mediterranean bowl. Rome paved, bridged, and wrote itself into stone, turning mare nostrum into a logistics engine: grain ships from Egypt, oil and garum from Spain and North Africa, taxes in coin and kind. Law, legion, and Latin (with Greek as the other half of the tongue) held a mosaic together; when the center shifted east to Byzantium, Greek courts, Orthodox liturgy, and gold solidi kept roads open long after old names cracked. At the edges, Rhine, Danube, desert, federates, and foes learned the playbook and rewrote it.
- India's corridors. Under the Maurya, Aśoka had edicts inscribed in stone and spread an ethic of rule that praised restraint and care for beings; later empires and kingdoms, Gupta in the north, Śātavāhana, Chalukya, Rāṣṭrakūṭa, Pāla, Chola elsewhere, made their own grammars. The Chola pushed power seaward: temples as treasuries, ships as messengers, copper plates as contracts. Inland, irrigation tanks and bunds wrote authority into water.
- China's dynastic weaves. The Qin unified script and axle width, set weights and measures, and stitched walls; the Han made a durable civil order, local magistrates, commanderies, salt and iron monopolies, tribute spun into bureaucracy, and roads flanked by post houses. Dynasties turned and returned, Tang, Song, Yuan, Ming, each revising the pact between court, scholar-officials, merchants, peasants, and frontier peoples. The state's great rivers, the Grand Canal, and later extensions, moved grain and the mandate.
- Southeast Asian mandalas. Empires here were often fields, not hard borders, with power strongest at the center, fading to influence at the edges. Angkor mirrored cosmos in waterworks and towers; Pagan seeded a plain with temples; Majapahit in Java, Ayutthaya in Siam, each drew islands and valleys into spheres of tribute and intermarriage, with harbors facing the monsoon and hinterlands fed by rice.

- The Sahel and savanna. West African empires, Ghana (Wagadu), Mali, Songhai, rose on gold, salt, and the savvy of the river and the desert. Mansas and askias ruled via lineages and offices; griots kept law in story; caravans crossed the Sahara's sea to markets that linked Timbuktu and Gao to Cairo and Fez. Farther south and east, Benin ringed its forest capital with earthworks; Ife cast brass faces like a living presence; on the plateau, Great Zimbabwe stacked stone without mortar into enclosures that spoke commerce and authority in the same breath. In the highlands to the east, Aksum traded across the Red Sea and minted coins while Christian liturgy took root in Geʻez; later, Ethiopian polities worked treaties and terraces in mountain light.
- The Andes and the mesh of roads. Wari and Tiwanaku showed how highland polities could feed cities with canals and terraces; later, the Inca bound four quarters with the Qhapaq Ñan, a road network stepped with tampus(way stations), rope bridges, runners changing at posts like a pulse. Tribute came as labor (mit'a) as much as goods; khipu, knotted strings, kept accounts, recorded census, and maybe more.
- Mesoamerican mosaics. City-states and empires rose and fell: Teotihuacán's shadow, Maya kingdoms in cycles of alliance and war, and later the Mexica (Aztec) Triple Alliance projecting power across central Mexico through tribute lists, market oversight, and ritual awe. Causeways and canals made lake cities walkable; pochteca merchants carried news and jade.
- The steppe and the hinge of worlds. Pastoral empires, Scythian, Xiongnu, Türk, Mongol, spanned grass oceans where walls looked like invitations. Chinggis Khan and his heirs made the fastest post network of their age (örtöö), enforced a stern order on highways, moved artisans like treasure, and kept a ledger of loyalties broader than any one law code. For a century and more, caravans crossed from China to the Mediterranean under passports stamped with a square of felt and a seal. The steppe was not "outside"; it was another center, mobile and memorized.

The edge as teacher

Edges are not empty. They are workshops where different ways of life negotiate plow and herd, mountain and plain, sea and land, city and village. Edges make:

- Middlemen cultures. The Swahili coast, Nabataea, and later Palmyra in desert belts, Oasis towns on caravan lines, border marches in Europe, Kashmir, and Yunnan as hill-valley interfaces, places that speak two or three economic and ritual languages at once.
- Hybrid law. Frontier courts mix tribal codes, imperial statutes, and custom. A pastoral raid can be settled by cattle, coin, oath, or marriage, depending on who stands watching. A sensible empire lets plural law run so long as grain and peace arrive.
- New peoples. Edges welcome fugitives and ambitious novices: soldiers taking wives and fields, clerks learning local scripts, artisans whose skills outrun guild rules at the center. Diasporas, Armenian, Jewish, Indian, Chinese, Arab, African, build leagues of trust that survive dynasties.

The arts of legitimacy

Empire must speak why. It does so with:

- Genealogy and myth. Founders descend from gods or heroes; banners carry emblems with long shadows; capitals perform cosmic geometry.
- Ritual and mercy. Coronations, amnesties, the freeing of prisoners at festivals, public granary openings in famine, staged benevolence is also logistics.
- Law and learning. Codes carved in stone; schools that teach the center's script; exams that turn ambition into bureaucracy; tax remissions that reset economies without admitting failure.

- Art and monument. A road that drains well is propaganda you can walk; a tower that does not fall in an earthquake is a sermon about care.

Extraction, care, and revolt

Empires take: land, labor, sons, daughters, timber, ore, time. The best also give: flood relief, safe roads, fair weights, courts with appeal. The line between tax and theft is often the line between longevity and collapse. When rulers mistake a people for a quarry, taxes become ransom, and rebels find roads already laid for them. Revolt is a language the poor speak fluently; so is evasion, the everyday arts of the weak: false weights, late sowing, quiet flight to hills and forests, selective deafness to orders that insult custom.

The view from inside a ledger

A dynasty's pride sits in numbers: so many households, such revenues, such granaries filled, such men under arms, such miles of wall. But a ledger cannot show how a village endures: whose sheaves fed whose oxen in drought, which 'uncle paid a nephew's tax after the father died, which woman's beer kept a work gang loyal to a foreman who listened. Empires count; societies survive.

Women and the work of state

The archive names kings and generals; the ground remembers women as officials, patrons, entrepreneurs, weavers, brewers, estate managers, priestesses, healers, regents, wives who kept lineages coherent across treaties. Letters show them arguing cases, directing shipments, funding shrines and schools. Inheritance rules and marriage contracts were not only private matters; they were engines of state. When the center noticed this and protected women's property and mobility, whole regions steadied.

War and its limits

Empires fight from habit. Yet even war has rituals: seasons for campaigning; truces for harvest; embassies with food under white flags; rules about temples and markets. Some codes are cynically broken; some are surprisingly kept. The edge between "raiding economy" and "steady trade" is thinner than we admit; a good road tempts both.

How ideas travel in harness

An empire with post houses not only moves troops. It moves philosophy, art, and faith. Monks ride roads first built for tribute; jurists' notebooks circulate with salt; a new meter of poetry thrills a port, then a court; cuisine changes in the palace and trickles out to alleys. When centers fall, the corridors remain. Later powers inherit the channel and pour new wine into old amphorae.

How we know (notes from the toolkit)

- Roads & posts. Stone mile markers, stamped bricks, culverts, bridges with repairs; ruins of post houses littered with horse bones and feed bins; dispatch sticks and seals.
- Paper trails on pliable media. Ostraca and bamboo slips, birch bark and papyrus, parchment and paper; charters hoarded in monasteries and mosques; copperplate grants; receipts in storeroom jars.
- Coins & measures. Standard weights with official stamps; coin hoards that narrate panic and reform; metrological tables on school tablets.
- Waterworks. Canals, cisterns, stepwells, aqueducts, bunds, and tanks; silt patterns that show neglect; pollen that maps crop change.

- Walls & frontiers. Ditches, ramparts, signal towers, forts; burnt layers that write a raid; villages rebuilt one terrace upslope after an edict changed a border.
- Voices. Chronicles, petitions, court records, letters, especially the small ones where a widow asks remission or a garrison complains about moldy grain.

Motif across worlds: Road and Wall

Empires draw two lines: a road to carry life and a wall to say "not here." Many roads become the next age's commons; many walls become quarries. The wise ruler learns which to lengthen and which to lower. A telltale of decline is the wall grown higher while the road grows weeds.

Three scenes from the seams

- A steppe market at dawn. Felt tents circle a corral; ironwork from a city two weeks away glints on a saddle; a tax collector with frost in his mustache haggles over sheep he cannot count at a glance. A singer warms his voice; his song will settle a quarrel better than the collector's stick.
- An inspection at noon. On a canal, a minister stoops to taste silt, too much, orders crews to dredge, writes three names, and cancels two tax arrears. A girl on the bank watches the water change color as mud rises; she will remember the day a man with a brush and a voice moved a river.
- A fort at dusk. The watch lights a beacon; someone answers down the chain. In the yard, a conscript mends a sandal with a borrowed awl; he hums a tune from home while a scribe counts arrows and a cook thickens lentils with yesterday's bread.

Costs and gifts

Empire costs: conquered neighbors, coerced labor, provinces drained for a capital's delight, languages trimmed, old gods demoted, bodies broken on walls. Empire gifts: roads that still carry food, weights that still keep markets honest, schools that teach peasants' children to read their rights back to officials, aqueducts that still give water. The historian's task is to hold both without blinking.

Afterimage

Night lays a calm hand on milestones, terraces, and river steps. The post road empties. A fox crosses where an envoy rode at noon. In a city that once set the calendar for a continent, bats skim a dry cistern; not far away, women in bright clothes queue at a spigot to fill blue plastic jerrycans fed by a pipe that remembers the slope of a Roman conduit. The empire is gone; the habit of passage remains. Tomorrow a bus will follow the old road's curve around a hill the way a satrap's courier did, and the land, patient, long-memorized, will shrug and carry another load.

PART VII: COLLISIONS & CREATIONS

CHAPTER 20

1492 AND ITS REVERBERATIONS

A canoe noses into a bright Caribbean bay. Children on shore point: a floating house with cloth wings. The strangers climb down a ladder into the shallows, metal gleaming at their belts, a banner snapping like a bird. A woman shades her eyes. Somewhere behind her, cassava cakes cool on a stone. In the strangers' wake come animals that have never grunted on this sand, seeds that have never sprouted in this soil, and a fever that has never burned in these bodies. The world is about to join, and break, in ways no one there can imagine.

Before the year that became a symbol

"1492" is a doorframe, not a wall. Before it, continents already pulsed with their own highways, Silk Roads, Indian Ocean monsoons, steppe corridors and river webs. After it, a single biosphere emerges: plants, animals, people, microbes, metals, and ideas cross oceans that had long kept them apart. This is the century when oceans stop being edges and become rooms inside one house.

Seeds, beasts, and fevers: the great exchange

What later scholars called the Columbian Exchange was not a trade agreement; it was an ecological collision. Some of what moved, and what it did:

- From the Old World into the New: Horses, cattle, sheep, pigs, goats, muscle, milk, wool, and hooves that remade landscapes and diets; wheat, barley, rice, sugarcane, coffee, bananas, citrus, fields, and plantations that changed work and taste; the honeybee, a quiet colonist. Along with them came microbes, smallpox, measles, influenza, later malaria and yellow fever, that tore through unexposed populations. Villages emptied in waves, the conquerors mistook for victories of steel.

- From the New World into the Old: Maize, potatoes, cassava, tomatoes, chili peppers, cacao, peanuts, squash, pineapple, tobacco, vanilla, foods that filled bellies and fancies from Ireland to India, from the Congo to China. A potato up a hillside could feed a family where wheat would fail; maize made new bread in Africa; cassava became famine insurance. These gifts thickened Eurasian and African populations, an irony next to the losses across the ocean.
- On debate and care: The origin of some diseases (notably syphilis) remains debated; the point here is not to settle that file but to mark how uneven the exchange felt: one side received new staples; the other, often first, received new plagues.

Ecology remembers. Horses remade the Plains and the Pampas. Pigs rooted up Indigenous gardens and went feral. Sheepstripped valleys to dust where grazing outran restraint. Weeds rode in fodder and ballast. Forests fell for sugar and ship timbers. And yet people adapted: terraced milpas adjusted to steel tools; cacao learned convent kitchens; chilies married Sichuan pepper.

Conquest, alliance, survival

The first islands, Hispaniola, Cuba, Puerto Rico, taught Europe what conquest might mean: encomiendas that bound Indigenous communities to labor and tribute; missions and forts; epidemics that arrived ahead of auditors and laws. On the mainland, empires fell not to single swords but to coalitions and contagions. In Mesoamerica, tens of thousands of Tlaxcalans and other Indigenous rivals helped topple the Mexica (Aztec) Triple Alliance; in the Andes, civil war within the Inca world and successive epidemics made Spanish victory thinkable. In both Indigenous strategies, alliance, evasion, uprising, and litigation never ceased. The archive is full of Indigenous petitions, maps, and court cases: survival through the pen as well as the lance.

Colonial rule varied by place and time. The Spanish crown debated the humanity and rights of Indigenous peoples in hearings and laws (Laws of Burgos, the Valladolid debate), imperfect shields that sometimes softened blows, but often didn't. Reducción projects moved communities into planned towns; mita labor drafts in the Andes fed mines and mills; mission systems entwined conversion with new economies. In Portuguese and later Dutch, French, and English spheres, other grammars governed, but the sentence often read the same: extraction with doses of reform and resistance.

Sugar, silver, and the chained road

Two things turned oceans into engines: sugar and silver.

- Sugar loves heat, water, and labor in great quantities. Plantations in Brazil and later the Caribbean devoured forests and people, grinding cane into wealth for ports across the Atlantic. To feed that machinery, merchants and rulers built the Atlantic slave trade, kidnapping, selling, and forcing the transport of millions of Africans. The Middle Passage was not a line; it was a wound. Those who survived carried languages, gods, drum patterns, farming knowledge, ironwork, recipes, and names, many forcibly changed, into new worlds. They also carried resistance, from daily slowdowns to maroon communities in forests and hills (quilombos, palenques) to revolts that shook empires.
- Silver flowed from Zacatecas and Potosí, a mountain turned hive, down llama trains and mule paths to ports, across to Seville and Lisbon, and, crucially, through Acapulco onto Manila galleons bound for China. There, silver met a hungry tax system and a silk industry; coins and bars became silk and porcelain that rode back to Mexico and Peru. For the first time, a miner's pick in the Andes could move a bolt of cloth in Suzhou. The world had a single money loop.

Mercury from Huancavelica and Almadén made silver run: amalgamation turned ore into quick profit, and poisoned valleys and workers alike. The ledger of early globalization is written in coins, yes, and also in blue fingers and damaged rivers.

Converts, crossings, and new saints

Missionaries walked and sailed with soldiers and merchants: Franciscans, Dominicans, Jesuits, Augustinians, Moravians, and others learned local languages, compiled grammars and catechisms, argued with colonists about cruelty, saved lives, and sometimes erased names. Conversion in the Americas and Africa rarely meant simple replacement. Syncretisms flourished: Guadalupe in Mexico braided local reverence with Marian devotion; in Brazil and the Caribbean, Candomblé, Umbanda, and Vodou dressed African deities as Catholic saints to protect them in sight; in the Andes, mountains wore crosses and kept their ancient authority.

In Asia, missions met strong states and old religions. Jesuits at the Ming–Qing court translated Euclid and studied rites; in the Rites Controversy, Europe argued over how much Confucian practice a Christian might keep. Converts became mediators and sometimes martyrs. The age of crossings made comparative religion a lived problem.

New foods, new peoples, new worlds

A farmer in Ireland plants potatoes in poor soil and survives a winter that wheat would have failed. A woman in Kongosells maize porridge by a road lined with oil palms. A peasant in Bengal adds chili to a lentil stew; in Sichuan, chilies meet peppercorn for a new tongue-tingle. Chocolate, sweetened with cane, moves from a Mesoamerican ceremonial drink to a European breakfast cup; coffee from Ethiopia–Yemen routes becomes a Paris and London habit; tea travels deeper into British veins; tobacco smokes across class and continent.

Meanwhile, mestizo, mulatto, criollo, and other caste names multiply on colonial forms, trying to pin identity like a butterfly. People lived more fluidly than the lists. Families knitted across lines; languages mixed into creoles; new nations would one day grow from these households.

Maps, measurements, museums

The encounter remade knowledge. Cartographers stitched new coasts onto old parchment; botanical gardens in European capitals grew global collections; cabinets of curiosity sorted shells, idols, insects, skulls, beauty, and violence in drawers together. Printing presses in Mexico City and Lima made local texts; Indigenous painters and scribes recorded histories in hybrid scripts and images; African and Asian scholars corresponded with Europeans about medicine, law, and astronomy. Out of this mess and brilliance would come both modern science, with its instruments and methods, and the racist taxonomies that would justify theft for generations. That tension is the next chapter's work.

Resistance and revolution on Atlantic winds

If oceans carry cargo, they carry ideas. Languages of rights, reason, and redemption rode with ships and sermons. Enslaved people on Saint-Domingue (Haiti) listened, remembered older vows, and rose. Their revolution (beginning in 1791) became the fulcrum of an age: the only successful slave revolt to found a lasting state, a beacon and a terror to empires built on sugar. Elsewhere, maroons signed treaties; Indigenous confederacies fought and negotiated; colonists' children, criollos, read European philosophers and declared republics. The age that Columbus's ships opened closed, temporarily, with anti-imperial storms no one in that first canoe could have guessed.

What did it feel like?

- On a plantation dawn. A woman wakes before the drum. She thinks in two languages at once, neither a secret to her. She ties a cloth the way her grandmother did across the sea and sings a line that isn't written down anywhere. She plans a meeting at the edge of the cane where the ditch curves.
- In a highland mine. A man's breath steams in cold air underground. He counts strokes to keep from swearing and from crying. At night he will chew a bitter leaf to forget his back. He knows a prayer to a mountain that the priest calls a saint; he says both.
- In Manila. A broker counts silver reals and stacks silk bolts. He jokes with a man from Puebla about chilies. A printer across the street sets type in three scripts. A sailor sleeps on deck with a rosary his African mother put in his pocket. The wind decides if anyone's plans matter.

How we know (notes from the toolkit)

- Ships & ports. Wrecks with cargoes of coins, porcelain, cacao, sugar; ballast stones that betray routes; dock timbers and customs ledgers; port ordinances and guild records.
- Bones & seeds. Isotopes in human remains that show childhoods spent elsewhere; pollen and phytoliths tracking crop arrivals; pig and cattle DNA tracing feral herds; parasite eggs in latrines telling of disease.
- Codices & chronicles. Indigenous painted books and alphabetic texts; petitions and maps drawn for courts; missionary grammars; plantation ledgers; manumission papers; runaway notices; Inquisition trials that inadvertently preserve everyday speech.
- Landscape scars. Terraces reworked for wheat and barley; charcoal layers from sugar mill fires; mercury in lake sediments; cattle trails etched into new grasslands.

Boundaries & care

Telling this story requires two guardrails:

- Agency and atrocity together. Neither "inevitable progress" nor "pure catastrophe" does justice. People suffered, acted, adapted, resisted, and created. We name genocide and enslavement plainly, and also name survivance, the active endurance of cultures that refused to die.
- Local specifics. "The Americas" and "Africa" are not monoliths; Caribbean isles differ; West and West-Central African societies differ; empires are not the same as their colonies. The book keeps names and dates close to places.

Motif across worlds: Seeds & Chains

Two objects define the age: a seed and a chain. The seed promises a future folded small, potato eye, maize kernel, cane cutting, able to feed millions or enrich a few. The chain measures a theft of time, of kin, of motion. Much of the next century will be the struggle to plant without binding, to keep the gift of exchange, and end its shackles.

Afterimage

Night in a harbor. Lanterns throw ovals on black water. On one pier, barrels of sugar leak a molasses shine; on another, bundles of cacao smell like earth and thunder. In a lane uphill, a woman folds a small braid into a child's hair the way her mother taught her, the way it was done on a different coast. In a monastery cell, a friar crosses out a line in a sermon and writes "neighbors" where he had written "savages." Out at anchor, a sailor holds a coin and feels the stamp with his thumb. He does not know that the coin will end up melted in a far city and that the mercury that helped mint it will linger in a river his great-grandchildren drink. He falls asleep. The tide turns. A rat decides which ship to board. The world, hinged on water, swings again.

CHAPTER 21

NEW SCIENCES, NEW CHAINS

A man leans over a table where glass and brass gleam. A candle throws light through a lens; the lens shows a flea as tall as a horse, armored and jointed, a monster from a puddle. In another room, a tube of mercury drops when a storm nears; in another, a clock with a heavy bob keeps steadier time than any prayer bell. On a headland, two watchers time the Transit of Venus to fix the scale of the solar system; on a deck, a carpenter's son winds a marine chronometer so a ship can know its place in an ocean without landmarks. Curiosity finds a toolkit and a method, instruments, experiments, replication, print, and calls itself new science.

Across the water, a drum starts in the dark. A bell, iron or wooden, governs when bodies wake, cut cane, haul, boil, and sleep. A book on a desk in a counting house lists barrels of sugar and names of people bought and sold. Another book, polished leather, gilt, classifies plants in neat Latin, clipped from latitudes where the book's author never sweated. Curiosity and cruelty develop in tandem. This chapter keeps them in the same frame.

A method, and its rooms

In the 1600s and 1700s, philosophers and mechanics made labs out of kitchens and cellars. They heated and weighed, measured and recorded; they agreed on procedures and argued in letters; they founded societies where experiments were performed before witnesses and then printed so strangers could repeat them. A fragment of a new grammar took hold:

- Instrument: lens, pump, balance, prism, thermometer, barometer, quadrant, later the chronometer, trustworthy extensions of the senses.

- Replication: the same steps yield the same result; a fact is a habit the world keeps.
- Publishing: journals and proceedings knit a conversation; priority matters less than showing your work (and, humanly, often matters more).
- Dissent: argument is not treason; it is how a claim hardens.

Telescopes made the Moon a world; microscopes made rot a city; an inverse square law turned orbits from epicycles into ellipses; chemists unhooked air into gases and weighed invisible worlds. The point here is not who did which theorem; it is that many places learned to turn wonder into procedure.

Gardens, voyages, paper empires

Empires grew botanical gardens the way they raised forts. Kew near London, Calcutta on the Hooghly, Pamplemousses in Mauritius, Bogor near Batavia: living libraries where plants were collected, named, propagated, and shipped. A breadfruit cut from Polynesian stock crossed the oceans to the Caribbean to feed enslaved workers; cinchona bark from Andean forests, the source of quinine, was smuggled to seed plantations in Java; tea plants and secrets left China for India under guard and guile. A map of root systems mirrored a map of trade winds and flag colors.

Naturalists sailed on survey ships and came back with crates: shells, skins, seeds, rocks, notebooks, Indigenous words. Taxonomy offered a clean, two-word Latin for a world of messy names. Herbaria pressed leaves flat to be read in Europe; museums arranged bones and idols into stories that flattered the buyers of tickets. Cabinets of curiosity, the old Wunderkammern, gave way to public halls that promised universal knowledge and hid the cost of how it was gathered.

Much of this knowledge arrived in European languages born elsewhere: Incan farmers teaching terrace and frost avoidance;

Andean and Quechua healers pointing out bark that calmed a shaking fever; West African experts in rice irrigation transforming Carolina swamps into paddies; enslaved artisans making mills run and iron flow; sailors from Malabar and Fujian piloting monsoon and reef for foreigners rich and quickly promoted. Inside the Latin binomial, a thousand unnamed teachers disappear.

Companies and chains

Alongside academies, chartered companies, VOC, EIC, and others carved out commercial states. They minted coins, raised armies, made treaties, ran courts, and planned monocultures that turned soil and water into spreadsheets. Silver and spice were not metaphors; they were ledger lines. In Bengal, revenue (tax) flowed through company hands, where climate and policy collided, famine stalked villages, while warehouses held grain for export. On coasts and islands, sugar estates devoured seasons and bodies; to feed them, the Atlantic slave trade packed holds with people.

The plantation was a laboratory with a whip: efficiency measured in lashes and boils; time discipline enforced by drum and bell; lives converted to output; overseers keeping double books when the law or conscience peered in. Techniques moved between fields and factories: the boiling house inherits the language of the brew house; the mill prefigures the manufactory where other bodies will later stand the same length of day.

After abolition laws began to close the transatlantic trade and, in some empires, slavery itself, new coercions replaced old ones: indenture drew workers from India and China to sugar, tea, and rubber; convict labor built roads and towns; debt peonage bound families to mines and haciendas. Chains rust and are recast.

Coal, cotton, steam

In rain-smoked valleys and brick-walled towns, water wheels and steam engines gathered work into buildings called mills. Cotton, grown by enslaved people in the American South and elsewhere, fed looms in Lancashire; cloth returned to West African and Asian markets where other weavers had once held the trade. Coal blackened lungs and skies and freed workshops from riverbanks. Railways and telegraphs stitched territories into clock time: noon struck when wires said it should. Factory whistles inherited the plantation bell's pedagogy: hours into orders.

New sciences rode these rails: thermodynamics and statistics began as ways to talk about engines and populations; vital statistics and censuses made governments count lives and deaths as if they were pressure and volume. Numbers would be used to save lives, the sewer, the vaccine, and to rationalize their ordering, the workhouse, the pass.

Race as a technology

Classification's bright promise grew a shadow. Out of measurements and museums came racial typologies, craniometries, and theories that arranged people in ladders. Phrenology peddled skull bumps as destiny; "scientific" treatises stitched prejudice to Latin. Human remains collected without consent sat in drawers; "specimens" of culture and body fed expositions where visitors consumed human difference as entertainment. Race hardened into a technology of rule: who may own, vote, testify, migrate, marry.

At the same time, opponents used the tools of the new sciences to unmask them: data on slave ships and disease; exposés of mining camps; abolitionist pamphlets that tallied suffering; missionaries' and travelers' ethnographies that complicated contempt; Black and Indigenous intellectuals who wrote histories, preached sermons, published newspapers, and composed novels and music that carried counter-knowledge into salons and streets.

Women at the bench, women at the wheel

Women appear in lab notebooks as assistants, translators, illustrators, funders, experimenters; in mills as weavers, spinners, inspectors, organizers. They mapped seaweeds and comets, kept observatories and gardens, ran pharmacies and printing presses; they also filled boarding houses of factory towns and sent wages back to farms. Some published under their own names and paid for it; many more did not. New sciences traveled on gendered labor, exposed when strikes and petitions made it visible.

Faith, reason, and the street

The age of experiment did not erase devotion. Many researchers wrote prayers before papers; many preachers studied astronomy and natural history with seriousness. Revivals and awakenings swept countries feeling the factory's drag; millenarian hope flickered where contracts and clocks left little room to breathe. New scriptures of reason and rights were staged in constitutions and guillotines, moral imaginations widened and narrowed in the same rooms.

Resistance and re-imagining

Where chains tightened, people answered. Maroons carved free space in mountains and swamps; Luddites smashed frames not because they hated machines but because they knew whose stomach the savings fed; strikes and friendly societies trained workers in solidarity; quilombos and palenques kept languages and gods alive; petitions to parliaments and courts produced awkward victories and necessary records. The very habits that made new sciences formidable, association, publication, and measurement, were repurposed by those who refused to be turned into numbers.

Three rooms in the same day

- A laboratory. A woman holds a prism and watches a beam break into colors she has learned to name by wavelength; she writes down the angle where violet breaks away and thinks of rain.
- A boiling house. A man stirs a copper with a wooden oar; the syrup at his feet crusts black. He has burns on both arms; he has a way to sing pain into smaller shapes and pass the song along so the hour ends.
- A counting room. A clerk sharpens a quill and enters both the day's sugar and the day's inoculations. He has not noticed he has written two histories in one ledger: how a body was used and how a fever was refused.

How we know (notes from the toolkit)

- Lab notebooks & proceedings. Step-by-step experiments; instrument sketches; minutes of societies; letters that debate methods and results.
- Ship logs & garden labels. Coordinates, weather, crew lists; seed packets and tags that track plant transfers; smugglers' and officials' papers that show the contradictions of law.
- Museums & herbaria. Specimen tags with dates and places; acquisitions ledgers that name donors and sometimes the violence that made a gift possible.
- Plantation ledgers & court records. Names, ages, prices, punishments; petitions, suits, and manumissions; abolitionist pamphlets and Parliamentary inquiries.
- Factory rules & strike notices. Whistles and fines written into posters; broadsides calling workers to a green at dawn.
- Censuses & "blue books." Demographic tables; sanitary reports; epidemiology maps that track cholera to a pump and sunlight to vitamin D.

We weigh these together, attending to silences: whose hands touched the thing we can measure, and whose names were filed off.

Boundaries & care

This chapter praises the method without turning it into a myth. It names cruelty without erasing creation. The same decades that filled skies with comets and labs with gases also filled holds with people and valleys with stumps. To tell one without the other is to lie.

Motif across worlds: Measure and Bind

New sciences teach how to measure time, pressure, heat, and growth. Empires teach how to bind people, land, debt, and hours. Measurement can free (antisepsis, safe water, storm warnings) and bind (quotas, passes, racial charts). The moral craft is to measure without chaining, to use clocks and tables in service of relief, not domination.

Afterimage

Night in a mill town. A whistle blows; a loom's shuttle comes to rest; a girl rubs her wrists and looks out at the canal where water curls around a brick corner—night in a plantation barracks. Someone hums; someone tells a joke that needs no language; someone plans a run—night in an observatory. A man wipes a lens with breath, then with a cloth; he notes a cloud; he imagines the same stars looking down on ports he has never seen and on fields he has never walked. In a city very far away, a cabinet opens; a curator slides a drawer and reads a tag in a careful hand. A beetle sleeps under glass. A skull does, too—the candles gutter. The century turns.

PART VIII: THE PLANETARY CENTURY

CHAPTER 22

REVOLUTIONS OF WORK, STEAM, OIL, DATA

A whistle cuts the fog; a belt turns; a thousand shuttles begin to fly. A century later a badge pings against a reader; a robot arm blurs and a scanner blips each box. Another generation on, a woman opens a laptop at midnight and earns a few cents labeling images for a company on another continent. Work keeps changing its engines, its clocks, and its rooms, and with each change, it reshapes families, cities, borders, and the planet itself.

The second day: electricity and the assembly line

Coal and steam began the industrial turn; electricity and management made it relentless. In the early 1900s, time-and-motion study, stopwatch in hand, standardized tasks into beats that could be taught in hours and repeated for years. The assembly line at Ford's River Rouge became symbol and threat: wages high enough to bind, speed set from above, a body reduced to motions the line demanded.

Electric light changed night from a boundary to a shift. Mills and foundries ran longer; houses glowed; streets learned to stay busy. Electricity also shrank power: a motor at each machine, an appliance on each counter. A washing machine in a kitchen was a revolution, if the household's hours truly changed. Often the bar for "clean" moved upward, and unpaid care work stayed long while the factory day shortened by law and struggle.

Two wars; one toolkit

World wars were laboratories for organization: mass production of engines and penicillin; radar rooms and ration books; code rooms and convoy schedules. Women entered factories in great numbers; so did forced laborers under fascism and occupation. After 1945, the tools stayed: assembly, logistics, quality control, and statistical monitoring. So did the lesson that governments could plan at scale, for tanks when needed, for housing and schools in peace.

The managed century: states, companies, and the household

In many countries, the mid-20th century built a pact: welfare states that stitched safety nets (pensions, unemployment insurance, public health, and schooling), strong unions, progressive taxes, and infrastructure on one side; productivity growth, consumer goods, and suburban mortgages on the other. The pact was uneven and exclusionary in places, but it taught a generation to expect stability.

Elsewhere, new nations came out of empire with two competing playbooks: import-substitution (build at home, protect young industries) and export-led growth (sell to the world, climb quality quickly). Five-year plans wrestled with quotas; family firms learned to use banks and ministries; cooperatives and communes tried to square ideal and hunger. In East Asia, a "flying geese" pattern, Japan, then the Tigers, then China and Southeast Asia, moved industries along wages and skills; in parts of Latin America and Africa, debt and commodity price swings whipsawed plans. Everywhere, the household scaled up: appliances and contraception altered time and choice; schooling lengthened childhood and shortened certain kinds of child labor, while others were pushed out of sight.

The box that made the world small

In 1956, a truck trailer was lifted onto a ship as a single container. The box seems humble; it re-wrote the world. Standard sizes and cranes reduced theft, injury, and time; ports became robotic valleys of steel and light; inland dry ports tied mountains to seas. The just-in-time gospel, minimal inventory, parts arriving hours before use, and factories that stretched across oceans. A phone order in Rotterdam woke a stamping line in Shenzhen that woke a night shift in a trucking yard in the U.S. Midwest. The box also rewrote labor: dockworkers went from gangs with hooks to small crews in cabs; strikes moved from piers to software that scheduled berths.

Oil's century and its shocks

Internal-combustion engines made oil the blood of the modern economy: cars, planes, plastics, fertilizers, asphalt, war. In 1973 and 1979, supply shocks made queues and policy; prices spiked; gasoline Sundays went quiet; thermostats turned down; small cars sold. The lesson stuck: energy is geopolitics, not just physics. Petro-states built glittering capitals and debts; importing nations learned efficiency and new dependences. Plastics turned into oceans and landfills; fertilizers made harvests fatter and rivers greener with algae. Oil income further financialized economies; traders' screens began to move mines and wells as surely as shovels did.

From mainframe to cloud: the data turn

A room-sized computer used to fill a building; now a datacenter the size of a stadium serves a continent. In between came microchips, personal computers, mobile phones, and the internet. The office became a screen; retail a logistics problem; music a file; maps a platform watching us walk. Work learned new verbs: email, search, upload, commit, deploy. Some skills rose (coding, design, data analysis, marketing to a crowd); others were atomized into micro-tasks (click this image if it's a cat), paid by the thousand for cents.

Management became algorithmic. Warehouses timed steps between shelves to the second; delivery routes were optimized by software that did not drive the truck; call-center scripts changed based on a customer's predicted mood; ratings on platforms governed who got the next ride or room. Surveillance, the old factory foreman's eye, became invisible and totalizing: keystroke, badge swipe, GPS trail, webcam. The promise was efficiency; the risk was inhumanity measured to three decimals.

The work we hide care, migration, remittances

Through all these revolutions, societies rested on work they rarely counted well: care. Feeding and washing, nursing and listening, rearing children and steadying elders, off the books or underpaid, made every "productive" hour possible. As rich countries aged and women's paid labor rose, households solved the arithmetic through migration: caregivers and cleaners crossing borders, sending remittances home that built houses and schools far away while their own families learned to love by voice note and holiday. Global care chains stretched like supply chains and suffered the same risks: exploitation, precarity, paperwork as a leash.

The informal and the shadowed

For hundreds of millions, especially in cities of the Global South, work means informal hustle: street vending, motorbike taxis, home piecework, repair, recycling. It is an economy without protective paperwork. Shocks, pandemics, storms, wars, hit this world first and longest. Yet it is also where resilience is strongest: rotating credit circles, extended families, neighborhood associations, and religious networks stand in when banks and ministries are late.

Financialization and the spreadsheet empire

Late in the 20th century, money began to earn more than factories did. Pensions and sovereign funds hunted yield; companies learned to please a quarter's report more than a decade's plan; households became leveraged (mortgages, student loans, credit cards) and thus governable by interest rates. In boom years, cheap credit built housing and capacity; in busts, balance sheets strangled towns. The spreadsheet was not neutral; it was a constitution written in columns.

The green edge of work

As the century turns and the climate warms, work must change again. Energy systems tilt to wind, sun, storage, and smarter grids; mines move to cobalt, lithium, copper, and the politics of extraction re-ignite, who carries the cost, who reaps the return? Buildings need retrofitting; trains and buses need building; soils need healing; forests need guardians paid to keep carbon in trees and peat. The transition risks repeating old harms, new toxic tailings, and new forced labor, if ethics and law don't arrive with the cranes. Its promise is vast: jobs that repair what jobs once frayed.

What workers did, and do, about it

Workers did not ride these revolutions passively. They organized into guilds, unions, cooperatives, and professions; they bargained, struck, and built parties; they also left, formed diasporas, or started businesses that flipped the script. In the digital age, the repertoire extends: platform co-ops, open-source projects, data unions, worker centers for gig labor, supply-chain transparency campaigns, and ethical investor coalitions. None are silver bullets; all are schools that teach dignity in the new rooms of work.

Three shifts in the engine room

- Energy: from muscle to steam, steam to oil and gas, oil to electrons that increasingly come from wind and sun.
- Management: from foreman to stopwatch, stopwatch to algorithm.
- Network: from river to rail, rail to container, container to fiber, and back to ports, the old bottlenecks with new code.

Each shift favored certain regions and households, then moved on. The map of winners and the map of the next winners rarely overlap perfectly. That churn makes policy, education, safety nets, antitrust, public health, and migration law more decisive than any single invention.

A small world, a long day: three rooms

- A port crane at dawn. A driver climbs to a glass box that looks down on a chessboard of steel. A screen shows which container next; a spreader lowers with a hum she can feel through her boots. Somewhere in her town a bar has postcards from ships that used to take a week to unload; now the bar is a gym and the gym is empty at this hour.
- A garment floor at noon. Fans push hot air across tables; a woman's needle finds the same seam a hundred times an hour. The manager checks a tablet; the order is behind; the brand wants photos at 3 p.m. to prove compliance. The woman's sister in another country picks the kids up after school and sends a photo of a drawing, three people, a cat, a plane.
- A datacenter at night. Rows of servers exhale; a technician swaps a drive and checks a dashboard: millions of queries a second, most of them small. Somewhere not far away a wind farm's turbines tick; a battery hums; a river runs past a locked gate built in a different century for a mill that made wool and then paper and then nothing.

How we know (notes from the toolkit)

- Ledgers to dashboards. Factory books, payrolls, union minutes, household time-use surveys, national accounts that reclassify what counts as "work" and "growth."
- Ports & chains. Shipping manifests, AIS ship-tracking, container yard logs, trade statistics, customs seizures, and port labor records.
- Energy balances. Coal and oil production and consumption tables; grid dispatch logs; satellite night-lights that track electrification and crisis.

- Labor law & struggle. Court cases, strike votes, safety inspections, accident reports, health records, migration files.
- Oral histories. Dockworkers' slang, machinists' tricks, midwives' and cleaners' routines, memory that outlives paperwork.

We read these together, mindful of what they miss: unpaid labor, illegal hours, the quiet heroism of routine.

Boundaries and care

This chapter admires ingenuity and also names costs, bodies disciplined by clocks and quotas, towns hollowed by offshoring, rivers silted by mines, eyes and wrists worn by screens. It resists the myth of inevitability. Work is made and can be remade, by policy and by practice, by law and by refusal, by invention and by saying no to uses of invention that shrink the soul.

Motif across worlds: Loom, Engine, Cloud

Three images hold the last two centuries. The loom taught us to synchronize bodies and threads; the engine taught us to bottle power and set the day by whistles; the cloud teaches us to treat code as weather, ever-present, taken for granted, hard to govern. The thread through all three is relationship: who holds whom to the clock, who owns the fuel, who writes the algorithm, and in whose name.

Afterimage

A father finishes a night of driving and leaves a paper bag with fruit on a porch before his kid wakes. A coder merges a pull request and closes the laptop on a desk that used to be a sewing table. A farmer scans a QR code on a sack of seed and checks a weather app that reads satellites and barometers in cities she will never visit. In a small apartment, an elder turns on a kettle and listens for a caregiver's key; the kettle hisses; the door opens; two people greet each other by name. Work, again, becomes what it always was beneath the engines: the ways we keep one another alive.

CHAPTER 23

BORDERS & BELONGING

A line of people waits in a hall that smells faintly of coffee and photocopier heat. Above the counters: clocks for different cities, a poster about prohibited items, and a map with arrows. A child holds a folder with a birth certificate, a vaccination card, and a photograph in which he looks too serious for his age. When their number lights up, his mother steps forward and answers questions in a rehearsed order: name, place, and who will meet you at the airport. Behind the glass, a clerk stamps and slides documents back like returning small boats to a stream. A door opens. A family steps into a new jurisdiction.

Borders turn space into law. Belonging turns law into home.

Nation and state: two names that rarely fit perfectly

A state is a power with an address: territory, government, courts, taxes, and a monopoly on legitimate force. A nation is a story of kinship at scale: a people who imagine themselves as "we," even when most will never meet. Modern politics made the two shake hands, "one nation under one state", and then spent two centuries arguing when the fit is tight enough to be just.

Before this marriage, identity stacked differently: village and clan, guild and parish, empire and city. People were subjects more than citizens; borders were zones more than razor lines; frontiers were gradients of language and law. The modern state made borders visible and portable, on paper, then in pockets.

How lines hardened

Maps turned hills and rivers into ink; surveyors and treaties turned ink into fences and posts. In the 19th century, a simple invention, barbed wire, let states and settlers draw long, cheap lines across grasslands where wood was scarce. In some regions, colonial offices drew straight borders on small-scale maps, slicing through pasture and watershed, kin and caravan. Elsewhere, partitions carved through living regions, new lines on old roads, producing hurried migrations and rooms full of grief.

A wall is a sentence in masonry. Some walls brag, some plead, some tremble. Many are less about keeping "them" out than keeping "us" in, taxes contained, conscripts counted, ideas slowed long enough for censors to breathe.

Papers, please: the rise of documents

Once, a traveler carried letters of introduction. Then the world learned passports, first as polite requests, later as requirements with photographs and visas. War and revolution swelled the number of people with no documents at all. After World War I, the League of Nations issued Nansen passports for the stateless; after World War II, the 1951 Refugee Convention mapped rights for those fleeing persecution; after many wars and new states, the world still confronts the question a document poses and dodges: who belongs where, and who says.

Inside some borders, other borders grew: internal passports and residence permits; pass laws that policed movement by race or class; household registries that sorted entitlements. A modern identity can be as much a number as a name: birth certificate → school record → tax ID → voter roll → passport → biometrics. The upside is protection and access; the risk is exclusion by clerical fact.

Routes of leaving, routes of return

People move for work, safety, love, study, adventure, climate, curiosity, and eviction. A handful of recurring routes:

- Transoceanic leaps. Steamships made migration a timetable rather than a voyage of roulette. Manifests list names and ages; offices stamped admitted or detained; some doors opened with a relative's address, a clean bill, and luck; other doors swung in both directions.
- Indenture after slavery. As empires abolished the trade in enslaved people, they turned to contract labor: men and women from India and China signed years of work on cane, tea, and rubber estates across oceans, to be repaid, sometimes, by land, wages, or a return ticket. Communities formed where the contract ended and the life began.
- Guest workers and rebuilders. After wars, rich states invited temporary workers to lay bricks, lay tracks, and weld steel, often with the tacit understanding that many would stay. New neighborhoods learned new breads, songs, and prayers; new families learned hyphenated names.
- Refuge and exile. Persecution, partition, coup, genocide, failure of rains, flood of armies, people fled. Some were welcomed by neighbors with shared tongue; others lived years in camps that grew into cities with schools and markets; others crossed without papers and built lives in the shadow.
- Internal migrations. Borders exist inside states too: rural to urban, farm to factory, hill to coast. These flows remake families, diets, and speech. They also test policy: do benefits follow the person or stay in the village ledger?

Everywhere, chain migration knits routes: one cousin writes, the next comes, a third opens a shop that stocks a familiar spice and a cheap calling card. Remittances, money sent home, pay school fees, buy tin roofs, dig wells; in many countries, they exceed foreign aid by far. The emotional remittance flows the other way: care across distance, a phone held up to the light so a child can wave at a grandfather's face.

Refugee, migrant, stranger, neighbor

Words matter. A refugee flees a well-founded fear of persecution; an asylum seeker asks a state to recognize that fear; an internally displaced person has fled without crossing a border. A migrant moves for many reasons, sometimes chosen, sometimes forced by drought or debt. An undocumented person is not a criminal; they are a person without a document that a system demands.

Hospitality and fear fight a long duel in the same street. Ports, farms, factories, and families are built by newcomers; politics often turns welcome into theater, sometimes generous, sometimes cruel. Faiths and philosophies across the world instruct care for the stranger; economies often reward the opposite. The outcome is not foreordained. It is policy, culture, and daily choice.

Internal borders, invisible fences

Some borders do not run at the edge of a map. They live in zoning laws, school districts, red lines on bank maps, and checkpoints within a state. They live in papers demanded only of some, in accents read as proof or threat, in surnames that open or close doors. A passport can get you across an ocean and still leave you outside a neighborhood.

Technologies at the gate

Borders learned new tools: biometrics (fingerprints, iris scans), databases that can talk across ministries and continents, satellites and drones that watch deserts and seas, smart fences that detect a ladder's weight. Phones became maps and lifelines for people on the move, routes, weather, and numbers for lawyers and cousins. The same phone became a leash in other hands, location logs, social graph, and algorithmic suspicion.

Travel styles changed, too. Some people buy mobility, visa-free passports, investor schemes, and second homes. Others cannot leave their own district without a permit. The world's map of ease does not match its map of need.

Languages of belonging

Belonging is a practice. Newcomers learn to name things twice: kitchen, cocina; bread, roti; home, two places at once. Children translate for parents at clinics and counters; grandparents teach songs in languages the state does not examine in school. Some communities push for assimilation, one tongue, one flag; others cultivate pluralism, many tongues in one market, many flags on one porch. Most households do both: keep some things tight, let other things braid.

Belonging also needs law. Citizenship by birthplace or by blood, by oath or by decree, each has history and hazard. Tests and ceremonies make insiders by ritual; expulsions make outsiders by edict; amnesties convert the shadowed into the counted. A fair regime cares less where you were born than how you live with others now.

Diasporas: far, and at home

Diasporas are not just "away." They are here/there: merchants and makers who keep towns knitted across seas; religious networks that fund clinics and schools; artists and activists who transform old arguments and invent new forms. Sometimes diasporas become bridges for peace and trade; sometimes they become conduits for long-distance nationalism, hardening conflicts with money and media. Most days, they are ordinary: groceries that smell like another childhood; remittances sent; a funeral flown home for; a child who answers to two nicknames and both are true.

Camps and cities of waiting

Prolonged displacement turns tents into towns. A camp starts with tarps and ends with streets and schools; years pass; a generation grows up knowing only ration books and checkpoints, Wi-Fi and dust. Humanitarian systems try three “durable solutions”: return, resettlement, or integration where people are. Each is costly in money and politics; each can fail; sometimes the only honest option is to support life where it is, without pretending the wait will end soon.

Frictions and cure

Nativist politics promise safety by shrinking the circle. Sanctuary movements answer by widening it, church basements, city ordinances, neighbor networks, lawyers and teachers who carry a quiet toolkit. Good policy does not confuse border management with moral worth. It invests in asylum systems that work, pathways to status for those who live and contribute, labor standards that punish exploitation rather than the exploited, and local supports (schools, clinics, housing) that keep reception from becoming resentment.

Three lines in one day

- Checkpoint at dawn. A worker shows a pass to cross a bridge for a job. The guard glances at the photo, then at a scar the worker has carried since a childhood no document records. The line moves; the sun comes up behind cranes.
- Consulate at noon. In a city far from both her birthplace and her current home, a woman swears an oath with a hand on a small flag. She is learning the new anthem’s words phonetically; her cousin records on a phone; later, they will eat two dinners, one for each country.
- Neighborhood at dusk. In a grocery where you can buy pickles from one continent and spices from another, a boy translates a

joke about soccer for an old man who never learned the new tongue. Laughter belongs without paperwork.

How we know (notes from the toolkit)

- Manifests & passports. Ship and plane logs, border cards, visa files, passport photographs, and applications, bureaucracies that accidentally become family archives.
- Censuses & surveys. Household counts, labor force and time-use data, remittance statistics; maps of schooling, health, and housing that show both welcome and neglect.
- Laws & cases. Nationality acts, asylum decisions, deportation orders, amnesties; court rulings that define who "belongs."
- Oral histories. Interviews at kitchen tables and in camps; songs, recipes, and festivals that carry memory across generations.
- Material traces. Suitcases, ID lanyards, camp ration cards, border signage; the design of fences and checkpoints; the footprints visible from the air where paths converge on a crossing.
- Digital trails. Phone records and social media groups used by migrants; NGO reports and satellite imagery tracking camps and boats.

We read these with consent and context, mindful that an archive can endanger the people it names if mishandled.

Boundaries & care

This chapter does not flatten violent and ordinary movement into one. Some people travel for school; others run for their lives. Some borders are lines on paper; others are rivers with bodies in them. We hold both truths and keep agency in view: people on the move are not freight; they are authors of their own decisions within constraints others often cannot see.

Motif across worlds: Door & Threshold

Every culture teaches a threshold ethic: who may knock, who must be let in, what the guest owes, what the host owes, and when the door must close. Borders are thresholds at scale. The motif's wisdom is old: announce your rules, keep your word, feed the traveler, punish the thief, and remember you were a stranger somewhere once.

Afterimage

Night at an airport. A janitor waves a mop under a bench where a man in a suit sleeps upright with his passport in his breast pocket like a small, rectangular heart—night at a desert fence. A boy watches a string of lights far off and whispers the few words of the following language he has learned from a cousin's phone—night in an apartment above a shop. A woman counts the day's cash, then counts the minutes until a video call, then counts the days until a festival she will celebrate with people on two continents at once. The map on the wall does not show any of this. Maps rarely do. Lives do.

CHAPTER 24

EARTH IN THE BALANCE

A boy falls asleep to the humming of a fan and wakes to the hush after a storm. On the window screen, a leaf sticks, then slides; the gutter speaks. In the kitchen, a grandmother turns on the tap and tastes the first minute of water to see if the city has remembered its work. Outside, the dawn smells faintly of smoke from a distant fire. The sky and the stone are talking at the same time. This is the century when we must learn to listen to both and answer.

A planet with vital signs

Earth keeps books. Carbon moves between sky and stone, leaf and ocean, a ledger written in sunlight and time. For long millennia, the entries were slow: volcanic breaths, buried forests, the tiny accounts of plankton shells raining down to the seafloor. In two centuries, humans found the deep pantry of fossil sunlight, coal, oil, gas, and burned it fast. The result is written plainly:

- Air holds more heat-trapping gases than it did before factories and furnaces multiplied.
- Oceans store the majority of the extra heat, expand as they warm, and grow more acidic as they absorb carbon.
- Ice on mountains and at the poles withdraws; sea level rises; storms ride warmer waters; downpours fatten and droughts bite.

Instruments make this more than mood: long air measurements that trace a rising sawtooth of seasons; ice cores with bubbles of ancient atmosphere; tree rings and lake muds that remember wet and dry; satellites that read sea height and forest loss; tide gauges that tick like careful clocks. The curves do not hate us. They merely show us ourselves.

Boundaries and thresholds

Imagine Earth not as a machine but as a patient with systems, circulation, lungs, and kidneys. Scientists speak of planetary boundaries: rough ranges within which the planet's life-support works in familiar ways, climate, biodiversity, nutrients (nitrogen/phosphorus), freshwater, land use, aerosols, ozone, and novel chemicals. Push far enough, and risks compound. Some changes arrive like a tide; others, like a tilt, the kind of turn you only notice after it has happened: a forest that becomes savanna; a current that slows; a sheet of ice that, once thinned past a line, keeps sliding even if the air cools later.

These are not prophecies. They are warnings written as probabilities. The sane response is not panic; it is prudence, to act before the hinge creaks.

Life in the ledger: more than climate

While the air warms, other books are out of balance.

- Species and places. Habitat shrinks; ranges shift; migrations miss their cues; many populations thin. Coral bleaches; insects, the quiet unsung majority, decline in some regions; large animals lose safe corridors.
- Water. Rivers are dammed, dredged, diverted; aquifers pumped faster than they fill; snowpacks feed fewer springs; coasts salt their own wells.
- Soils. Plows and chemicals have fed many and also worn out the land; carbon and life leak from fields that could be sponges.
- Nutrients. Fertilizer has turned hunger maps green and rivers green as well, blooms that choke lakes and coasts.

None of this denies the gifts of modernity, vaccines, safe water, where policy keeps its promise, and fewer children dying. It does say the bill is due: not for living, but for how we have lived.

Arithmetic and fairness

Not all hands have burned the same fuel. A small share of the world's people have produced a large share of the accumulated heat, and many who made the least are first to feel flood, heat, crop failure, and storm. This is climate not just as physics but as ethics:

- Responsibility. History matters; so does the capacity to change.
- Repair. Those who benefited most should shoulder more of the cost, cleaner energy built everywhere, loss-and-damage help when harm cannot be avoided, and debt relieved when interest smothers adaptation.
- Right to thrive. Ending poverty without repeating the smokestack path is the century's hard problem, and solvable if wealth moves as cleverly as data does.

Justice is not a garnish on climate policy. It is the recipe that keeps the meal from poisoning the guests again.

The tools on the bench

We already have workable tools, imperfect but enough to start anywhere:

- Cut the burn. Electrify what we can (transport, heat, many machines), feed that grid with wind, sun, water, geothermal, and, where needed, nuclear kept safe. Use less by wasting less: insulate, weatherize, tune motors, design for walking and transit.
- Clean the hard parts. For steel, cement, chemicals: efficiency first; then hydrogen, electrified heat, and capture only where alternatives are thin.
- Keep carbon in living things. Protect and restore forests, wetlands, peatlands, mangroves; farm and ranch so soils store more life; stop draining the ancient sponges.
- Adapt with care. Cool cities with shade and water; design buildings for heat; move out of floodplains and let rivers breathe;

restore dunes and reefs; build early-warning systems that reach the last mile.
- Aim standards at the system. Tighten efficiency codes, clean up supply chains, design products for repair; price pollution where it helps, police it where price fails; invest in public goods that markets underfund, grids, storage, transit, research.

Miracles welcome, fusion, better batteries, clever biomaterials, but not required to begin. The old builder's rule applies: use what you have, start where you are, make it better.

Stories and laws that help us remember

Cultures already carry ethics fit for a crowded planet:

- A sabbath for the land, fields that rest, gleanings left for the poor.
- Kaitiakitanga and other guardianship traditions that bind people to waters and forests as kin, not quarry.
- Satyagraha, ubuntu, ayni, and mutual obligation are named and practiced.
- New law from old insight: constitutions and courts that recognize rights of nature; rivers and forests granted legal personhood with human guardians to speak for them.

These are not slogans. They are institutions: councils, trusts, ceremonies, contracts. When joined to measurement and policy, they turn care into a durable habit.

Reasons for courage

We have done big things together and can again.

- The ozone layer was torn; nations banned the chemicals; the sky is healing.
- Cities that choked on smog cleaned their air in a decade when they chose to.

- Vaccination, sanitation, and green revolutions, each imperfect, each lifesaving, prove that numbers can be moved on purpose.
- Indigenous stewardship protects vast biodiversity with fewer fences and more relationships; community co-ops-keep lights on and bills down; debt-for-nature swaps and protected-area compacts show money can serve memory.

None of this erases grief already booked. It does say: agency beats cynicism.

Three repairs

- A river given room. A city buys out houses on a floodplain, turns streets into parks that drink; the next big rain runs green instead of brown. Children learn dragonflies' names in a place their grandparents called "the flood zone."
- A hot week that harmed less. Clinics stock salts and cool rooms; neighbors check on elders; bus stops get shade; employers move shifts; the heat record falls and the death record doesn't.
- A plant that retires. A coal unit winds down; workers take bridge pay and retraining; a battery and a peaker share the substation; the stack comes down like a bell rung backward. Someone keeps a brick.

How we know (notes from the toolkit)

- Air, ice, and rings. Continuous atmospheric CO_2 records; ice cores with trapped gas and dust; tree rings, corals, and speleothems tracing temperature and rainfall.
- Oceans and height. Argo floats and buoys take the ocean's temperature; satellites and tide gauges measure sea level; pH trends for acidification.
- Ecosystems. Remote sensing for forest cover, fires, and drought; field plots for species and biomass; eDNA that detects life from water samples.

- Health and risk. Heat-mortality statistics, flood and drought loss databases, crop yields, insurance and disaster records.
- Policy and practice. Emissions inventories; grid dispatch logs; building codes; treaty texts; court rulings where climate meets rights.

We braid these with local knowledge, fishing calendars, snow lore, fire sticks, and flood marks on a temple step. Evidence is fullest when instruments and elders agree, or argue in ways that teach.

Boundaries & care

Two temptations stalk this chapter: to doom (nothing matters) and to wish (technology will save us without change). Both dodge responsibility. The honest center says: we made much of this; we can unmake much; some will be lost; all the rest is up to courage and craft.

Motif across worlds: Sabbath for the World

Cultures everywhere prescribe rest, for bodies, for fields, for debts. The motif is not laziness; it is wisdom: limits make life possible. A planetary sabbath might look like habitats left uncut, species given corridors, mines that close with plan and pension, consumption slowed and sweetened, and time returned to relationships. Rest is not the absence of work; it is the right kind.

Afterimage

Night settles on a city whose river runs between new reeds. On a rooftop, a sensor posts the hour's air to a public site; in a basement, a freezer hums around vials that hold a century of pollen in order. A power plant glows with fewer stacks than it once had; a bus hisses past with a sound more like rain than an engine. On a coast, a wall of mangroves takes a small wave and turns it into lace. In a village, a woman notes that the spring is still singing in August and smiles the specific smile of someone who fought for a pipe and won. Above the roofs, a sky the color of the old sea holds a few stars that used to be just stories and are now also measurements. The boy who woke to rain is asleep again, one hand on a school notebook where he drew today's weather and tomorrow's plan. The fan is off. The window is open.

EPILOGUE, AFTER US?

Begin with two small scenes.

At dusk, a child kneels by a curb and draws a river with a stick where rain runs. She launches a leaf and names it after her grandmother. The leaf catches, turns, and goes. She learns a law with her hands: where water wants to go, it goes, and you can help it travel well.

At night, an old man steps outside and looks up. He knows the names of three stars and the season by their angle; the rest is simply company. He breathes in cold and lets it out warm and thinks, without words, I am part of this.

This book has tried to braid those two moments, stone and sky, measure and meaning, work and wonder, into one history of one humanity that refuses to be only one thing. After us, others will still read the same library. The question is what we leave in the margins.

What endures

Places endure. Caves that carry breath, pyramids that hold horizons, mountains that collect weather, tunnels that recall fear and care, rivers that remember each flood in a ring of silt, ice that keeps air like a locket. The ground stores the best and the worst of us without hurrying.

Practices endure. Counting beads, keeping sabbath, telling beginnings, reciting names, drawing lots, reading hands and stars, lighting lamps, closing the shop for a holy day, opening the gate for a stranger, setting aside the corner of a field. Techniques become rituals; rituals become law; law becomes habit.

Corridors endure. Roads and sea lanes outlast empires; recipes outlast borders; the wind returns; the monsoon remembers its turn; stick charts and star maps become GPS and still require a human patience to use well.

Questions endure. What is a person? What do we owe one another? How do we repair harm? How much is enough? What kind of power is safe to hold? How do we live with the dead and make room for the not-yet-born?

We cannot choose whether these endure. We can choose the condition in which the next people receive them.

What to pass forward (a small ledger)

1. Libraries, not monuments. Keep the places that teach, caves, springs, meadows, libraries, archives, observatories, open, legible, and cared for. A monument can be pride; a library is use. When you have to choose, choose the place where a child can learn.

2. Measures with mercy. Keep clocks, ledgers, maps, and data, and keep interpretation near them. Let numbers steer policy without excusing cruelty. The aim is relief: water that runs, air that heals, work that pays, borders that don't break families by accident or design.

3. Rest as law. Make sabbath large: for rivers that need room, soils that need cover, species that need corridors, bodies that need sleep, cities that need quiet. Idleness is not the point; proportion is.

4. Repair before wonder. Wonder is cheap and necessary, stars, cards, songs, a hand on stone. But if the roof leaks, mend it before you hold the concert. If the spring is tired, let it heal before you name it. If a story belongs to a people, ask before you tell it.

5. Plural on purpose. Refuse the single center. Keep many canons and kitchens, many calendars, many ways of saying "we." Plural is not a drift; it is a discipline: translation, patience, the habit of listening before naming.

6. Descent for return. We go under, into archives, tunnels, grief, and research, not to stay, but to bring something back: a law, a remedy, a song, a plan. The test of any descent is what it returns to the surface.
7. Work that keeps. Make jobs that repair roofs that breathe, grids that sip, trains that bind, forests that stand, care that is paid and prized. Teach skills that keep places livable, such as surveying, sewing, mending, growing, and coding that serve rather than extract.
8. Hospitality with teeth. Welcome is not a mood. It is policy, papers that can be had, wages that cannot be stolen, schools that teach newcomers without erasing their elders, streets where difference is ordinary and safe.
9. Tell the whole. In museums, syllabi, holidays, and films: pair achievement with cost, cruelty with resistance, collapse with re-growth. Name enslaved labor when you praise a harbor; name women's and migrants' work when you list inventions. This is not guilt; it is precision.
10. Leave room. In plans and parks and budgets and stories, leave margins for the unexpected student, the new bird, the festival invented next year, the drought we didn't expect, the discovery that asks us to change our minds. Rigidity is tidy; room is wise.

What to let go

Let go of the fantasy that one story can own the world. This book keeps company with assemblies, Anunnaki councils, synods, sanghas, senates, village elders under a tree, because power that speaks in a room is easier to answer than power that pretends to be the sky itself. The more we can move decisions from oracle to council, the longer we get to be wrong without ruining one another.

Let go, also, of the idea that the past was pure or the future will be. The past was mixed, brilliant, brutal, ordinary. So will the future be.

Our task is not to secure perfection but to raise the floor and lower the ceiling of harm.

A brief word to three readers

To the keeper. You carry ceremonies, archives, passwords, tools, and trails. Thank you. When you can, make an apprentice. When you must, say "no" and guard what should not be copied.

To the builder. You carry budgets, schedules, crews, and risk. Thank you. When you can, hire for repair. When you must, measure twice against the lives your plan will touch.

To the wanderer. You carry stories across lines, recipes across oceans, hopes across rooms where you are not yet at ease. Thank you. When you can, map back to where you began and forward to where your children will be at home.

A small liturgy of the everyday

- Touch stone: an old step, a lintel, a handprint if you are lucky. Remember, you stand in a long queue of hands.
- Look up: one star's name, one cloud's shape, one bird's path. Remember, the sky is a clock and a choir.
- Share bread: what was counted becomes common; what was sealed becomes sliced.
- Name a debt and forgive it if you can; name a harm and repair it if you can't forgive it yet.
- Leave one place better than you found it today: a ditch unblocked, a sink unclogged, a rumor corrected, a child answered well.
- Once a week, turn something off.

None of this is grand. That is the point. Civilizations are maintained by small, repeated acts. Cathedrals and canals, too, but mostly the daily keeping.

Last image

At the end of a long day, a person stands at a threshold, door, gate, trailhead, station, and listens. Behind them: a house that holds other sleepers, a ledger with the day's numbers, a table with crumbs and a folded cloth, a small jar where a cut flower leans. Ahead: a path into the dark that is not empty. A bat turns once. Somewhere, a server hums. Somewhere, a river slides its shoulder against a bank and remembers a flood from a century ago. Somewhere a child dreams a staircase made of light and another of stone, and in the dream, she knows they are the same ladder.

After us, others will walk out under the same sky and onto the same ground. May they find water that runs clear, roads that carry many, work that keeps life whole, councils that answer, stories that tell the truth, and rooms left for them. If they do, it will be because enough of us learned to read the world above and below, and to write back with care.

www.ingramcontent.com/pod-product-compliance
Lightning Source LLC
LaVergne TN
LVHW020716110826
845149LV00012B/2293